HOW TO READ THE BIBLE

How to Read the Bible

Richard Hall and Eugene P. Beitler
in association with
Dr. Francis Carr Stifler

J. B. Lippincott Company

Philadelphia   New York

CONTENTS

APPENDICES

Born in the East and clothed in Oriental form and imagery, the Bible walks the way of all the world with familiar feet . . . it has learned to speak in hundreds of languages to the heart of man . . . children listen to its stories with wonder and delight, and wise men ponder them as parables of life. It has a word of peace for the time of peril, a word of comfort for the day of calamity, a word of light for the hour of darkness . . . the wicked and the proud tremble at its warning, but to the wounded and the penitent it has a mother's voice . . . it has proven itself into our deepest affections and colored our dearest dreams; so that love and friendship, sympathy and devotion, memory and hope, put on the beautiful garments of its treasured speech . . . no man is poor or desolate who has this treasure for his own.

—HENRY VAN DYKE

AUTHORS' PREFACE

"How To Read The Bible" has been the title of many books, many chapters of books and countless leaflets, tracts and magazine articles. Some of these earlier treatments have been of a highly scholarly nature and almost all of them have been prepared for people already interested in Bible reading. This volume is possibly the first full-sized book ever prepared primarily for the person to whom the Bible is little more than a name: a book he has heard of, regarded with honor and respect, but never seriously considered reading.

There is little in these pages that will satisfy the critical Bible student or scholar. Footnotes have been sedulously avoided and even the citations of passages quoted from the Bible have been for the most part omitted. In a field where such an immense amount of research has been done and where so many differing opinions prevail, the abundance of generalities which fill these pages will raise many questions among earnest Bible students. The hope of the authors is that this very quality in their book will heighten its appeal to the person who is turning to the Bible for the first time or who may have grown discouraged in making a more scholarly approach to a projected program of regular personal Bible reading.

Above all it is our hope that these pages will be useful in turning many to a lifelong interest in Bible reading, which we believe is essential to the good life, to the preservation of those things which have made America a land of hope, and to the achievement of peace among the races and nations of men.

ACKNOWLEDGMENTS

In the preparation of this book, written neither by scholars nor for scholars, many scholarly books have been consulted. They are listed here, not only in grateful acknowledgment of their help but in the hope that many readers will go on to include them in their further study of the Bible.

In addition to these books, the authors are deeply indebted to *Sunshine Magazine* for permission to use part of its article, "The Lost Bible," as it appeared in *Religious Telescope* and to *Good Business Magazine* for permission to use Earl Perin's article, "Sales Aid." In addition, the authors are deeply indebted to the American Bible Society for freedom to consult its files and especially for permission to reprint as appendices some of its literature designed to encourage regular Bible reading; to use Dr. Clarence W. Hall's story of Shimabuku; and to quote from monographs prepared for the Society by the Reverend Joseph R. Sizoo and the Reverend John S. Bonnell.

We also wish to thank Dr. George Dahl, Holmes Professor of Hebrew Language and Literature, Emeritus, of the Yale Divinity School, who read the manuscript critically and made many helpful suggestions.

BOOKS CONSULTED:

Chamberlain, R. B. and Herman Feldman. *The Dartmouth Bible.* Boston: Houghton Mifflin Co., 1950
Chase, Mary Ellen. *The Bible and the Common Reader.* New York: The Macmillan Company, 1952

11

Dahl, George. *The Heroes of Israel's Golden Age.* New York: The Macmillan Company, 1923

Ferguson, Walter D. *Journey Through the Bible.* New York: Harper, 1947

Goodspeed, Edgar J. *How To Read the Bible.* Philadelphia: Winston, 1946

——. *How Came the Bible?* New York-Nashville: Abingdon-Cokesbury, 1940

Halley, H. H. *Pocket Bible Handbook.* Chicago: H. H. Halley (19th Edition, 1952)

Hamilton, Edith. *Witness to the Truth.* New York: Norton, 1948

Harper's Bible Dictionary. New York: 1952

Love, J. P. *How to Read the Bible.* New York: The Macmillan Company, 1945

Mould, E. W. K. *Bible History Digest.* New York: Exposition Press, 1950

Nelson, Lawrence E. *Our Roving Bible.* New York-Nashville: Abingdon-Cokesbury, 1945

Parmelee, Alice. *A Guidebook to the Bible.* New York: Harper, 1948

Paterson, John. *The Book That Is Alive.* New York: Scribners, 1954

Phelps, W. L. *Human Nature in the Bible.* New York: Scribners, 1922

——. *Human Nature and the Gospel.* Scribners, 1925

Simms, P. Marion. *The Bible in America.* New York: Wilson-Erickson, 1936

Stifler, F. C. *Every Man's Book.* New York: Harper, 1941

——. *The Bible Speaks to You.* New York: Greystone Press, 1948

Stimpson, George. *A Book About the Bible.* New York: Harper, 1945

The biblical quotations in this book are taken from the King James Version, the American Revised Version, the Revised Standard Version, the Smith-Goodspeed and the Moffatt Translations. Names of persons and places in the text follow the spelling used in the King James Version.

PART ONE

Why Read the Bible?

Chapter 1

"Honored Sirs, We Have Tried Our Best"

ONE DAY in 1945, Clarence W. Hall, a war correspondent following on the heels of our troops on Okinawa, came upon the tiny village of Shimabuku.

It was an obscure little community of only a few hundred native Okinawans. Thirty years before, an American missionary, on his way to Japan, had stopped here. He had not stayed long—just long enough to make a few converts, leave them a Bible, and pass on.

One of the converts was Shosei Kina, the other was his brother Mojon. From the time of the missionary's visit they had seen no other missionary and had had no contact with any other Christian person. But in those thirty years Shosei Kina and his brother had made their New Testament come alive. Picking their way through its pages, they had found not only an inspiring man on whom to pattern a life, but sound precepts on which to base a society.

Aflame with their discovery, they taught the other villagers until every man, woman and child in Shimabuku had become a Christian. Shosei Kina became head man in the village; his brother Mojon, the chief teacher. In Mojon's school the Bible was read daily. To Shosei Kina's village government, its precepts were law. Under the impact of this book, pagan

17

practices fell away. In their place, during these thirty years, there had developed a Christian democracy at its purest.

Then after thirty years came the American Army, storming across the island. Little Shimabuku was directly in its path and took some severe shelling. When our advance patrols swept up to the village compound, the GIs, their guns leveled, stopped dead in their tracks as two little old men stepped forth, bowed low and began to speak.

An interpreter explained that the old men were welcoming them as fellow Christians. They remembered that their missionary had come from America. So, though these Americans seemed to approach things a little differently than had the missionary, the two old men were overjoyed to see them.

The GIs' reaction was typical. Flabbergasted, they sent for the chaplain.

The chaplain came, and with him the officers of the Intelligence Service. They toured the village and were astounded at what they saw—spotlessly clean homes and streets, poised and gentle villagers, a high level of health and happiness, intelligence and prosperity. They had seen many other villages on Okinawa—villages of unbelievable poverty and ignorance and filth. Against these Shimabuku shone like a diamond in a dung-heap.

Shosei Kina and his brother Mojon observed the Americans' amazement and took it for disappointment on their part. They bowed humbly and said, "We are sorry if we seem a backward people. We have, honored sirs, tried our best to follow the Bible and live like Jesus. Perhaps if you will show us how . . ."

Hall relates that he strolled through Shimabuku one day with a tough old Army sergeant. As they walked the sergeant turned to him and whispered hoarsely, "I can't figure it—this kind of people coming out of only a Bible and a couple of old guys who wanted to live like Jesus!" Then he added a penetrating observation: "Maybe we've been using the wrong kind of weapons to make the world over."

Later, Clarence Hall held the Shimabuku Bible in his hand for a few memorable moments. At his request Shosei Kina reverently took it down from the pedestal where it rested, handling it with the loving care we would use with the original of our own Declaration of Independence. It was frayed and weather-stained. Its covers were almost off, its edges dog-eared from thirty years of constant use. This was the textbook of freedom that had made a new little world of Shimabuku.

What is this book which seems to have the power to re-mold people so near the image which has haunted all our dreams since the first Christmas?

The Bible is a book whose history and present influence in the affairs of the world make it the wonder of the ages. It is millenia old, but a best-seller today in the most progressive nations of the world. It is the product principally of the Jewish people, but has been read by more varied and remote groups than any other message ever written. Parts are so hauntingly phrased that they are memorized by thousands of people, yet all but a few scholars read it in a translation.

But there is a greater paradox than any of these. In spite of the enormous prestige the Bible has accumulated over the centuries, in spite of the power it has wielded in the lives of men and the praise it has won from leaders of government, art and religion, *it remains in America today the country's unread best-seller!*

As a selling proposition, the Bible simply has no serious rival. For a century it has outsold every other book in almost every country. The prospect is that in spite of any spread of totalitarianism it will always hold this high place. Today the Bible, in whole or in part, consistently sells more than twenty-five million copies a year, year after year, in more than six hundred languages. This is true not only in Christian countries but also in countries dominated by other faiths. In the United States it has outsold every other book every year since George Washington died in 1799.

But the gap between buying the Bible and reading it is huge: a gap many American families have never bridged. It is a book we have been taught to respect, but which few have removed from the shelf to explore. It is a book we have been assured can help us greatly, but to which few of us have opened our hearts.

Why should this be so? Perhaps because we are a prosperous people with access to countless books and seas of newspapers and magazines. The Bible is a long and difficult book. We hear it is a very great book, and we intend to read it sometime; but there are other books, new and timely books, books of required reading, short snappy books that people are recommending. We will read these first.

Then, too, there is ignorance of how to go about reading the Bible. Few parents are well enough posted to be able to help their children with it. They lack the time, energy and interest to absorb its wonders for themselves. Perhaps many of them have gone seriously about reading the Bible, but because it is a different kind of book, they have become confused and perplexed. Although the Bible has undoubtedly been for many people their greatest reading experience, for many others it presents a locked door.

Let us be just as practical and realistic as we can. How can these people be shown that the Bible is good reading? How can its reading become one of those experiences so engrossing that the sense of the passage of time is erased? Only when Bible reading is as much an adventure as reading a love story, watching a baseball game or spending an hour with a radiant personality, can it be truly rewarding.

Some of our interests are instinctive: for example, love between a man and a woman, family love. Other interests are of the sort that, although partially rooted in instinct, must be cultivated. The Bible is of this type. A "cultured" person is one who has deliberately cultivated certain interests that have enriched his whole existence. The really happy people in the world are those who have cultivated some interest until they have fallen in love with it; an interest in a garden, or a cote of carrier pigeons, symphonic music or astronomy or Shakespeare or amateur radio. These are the really happy people; but they have in every case had to put in some hard work to develop their interest. Their lives have been very different from the lives of that countless company of restless, dissatisfied, clock-watching Americans, who grudgingly go about their daily work and spend the rest of their time leaning their minds up against daily papers, picture magazines and other forms of entertainment that are, like spice, fine in small doses but disastrous if taken as life's principal spiritual food.

The Bible will not come to meet you nine tenths of the way. You must be prepared to take steps toward it. Like an automobile, its use must be mastered before you can expect it to take you anywhere. But also like your car it can take you to places you never dreamed of visiting.

If the book did not have this moving force, it would have been scrapped centuries ago, like almost every other sheaf of ancient writing. But no, every generation finds new power in the Bible, words that can move and mold their lives.

Some years ago an American engineer working for the government of India was sent on a surveying mission to the re-

mote northwest frontier of that country. As each evening
came on, his small party would head for the nearest oasis to
camp for the night.

One night, camped at a tiny oasis, he stepped outside his
tent after dinner to find a group of natives gathered. They
had heard that a government official had arrived and imag-
ined that he had a message for them.

The American engineer, a deeply religious man, felt
strangely moved as he stood and looked at the company of
natives. He was six weeks out in the desert, one hundred and
eighty trackless miles from any town and halfway around
the globe from America.

Before he realized it, the lonely engineer had started to
talk to the group squatting before his tent in their own language, which he knew fairly well. His talk turned, naturally
it seemed, to fundamental questions: the purpose of his
existence, and the destiny which had brought him to this
remote corner of India.

His audience listened without stirring and their absorption
encouraged him to go on. He spoke of universal brotherhood
and love. And finally he found himself describing man's age-
old yearning for God.

When he finished, an old man stepped forward. He was a
tribal prince with a long flowing beard. He came up, leaning
on his staff, as the young men courteously made way. He
looked at the surveyor, his strong face alert in the bright
moonlight.

He said, "You are a young man, and yet the things you
have been talking about—how do you know these things?
How do you know them?"

"Father," the American answered, "I don't know these
things because of my own personal wisdom. These are ques-

tions which have troubled human hearts since the beginning of time, and they have been answered in a book."

"Do you mean there is a book with all these things you have been telling us about?"

"There is such a book."

"Young man, you speak my language. Is this book also in my language?"

"It is, and I have it in my tent."

The old man straightened up and pointed his finger at the surveyor. "Get me that book!" he said.

The surveyor ran back into his tent and brought back two copies of the Bible. Forty brown hands were stretched out for them as he returned. He put one into the chieftain's hand. The old man took it and leafed through the pages.

"Tell me, young man, how long has this book been in the world?"

"For several thousand years."

"Did your people have it?"

"Yes."

"I am an old man. All my friends have died. I am nearly gone myself. And all this time the book was here and nobody brought it to me. *Why didn't someone bring us the book long ago?*"

The Second World War taught many Americans that the Bible was a book with living powers. One paratrooper said that whenever he faced a jump from his plane, this verse always occurred to him and soothed his nerves:

For I am persuaded that neither death, nor life, nor angels, nor principalities, nor powers, nor things present, nor things to come, nor height, nor depth, nor any other creature, shall be able to separate us from the love of God, which is in Christ Jesus our Lord.

This is from a letter that the Apostle Paul wrote to the congregation of new Christians in Rome, nineteen hundred years ago.

A naval lieutenant who had been rescued from his plane after it had plunged into the Pacific was later asked, "What did you think as you fell downward toward the sea?" "Oh," replied the officer, "I just repeated to myself, as I have been doing all my life when things get out of hand, 'The Lord is my shepherd; I shall not want. . . . Thy rod and thy staff they comfort me. . . . Surely goodness and mercy shall follow me all the days of my life: and I will dwell in the house of the Lord forever.'" The lieutenant had found strength in parts of the Twenty-third Psalm.

Other testimony by service men and women proves that the Bible kept them from being afraid.

Ken was a young officer in the American Air Force. One night his Flying Fortress failed to return from a bombing mission. It was reported shot down. Finally, word came to America that Ken had been taken prisoner in Italy with several other members of the bomber's crew. When Italy was defeated the Americans were allowed to escape, but German soldiers were everywhere.

Ken and his crew made their way into the mountains until they could get the lay of the land. They dared not approach any village, for they were literally surrounded by the enemy. At night they raided Italian turnip patches and provided themselves with rotten turnips which the farmers had left in the fields. By night they crept ahead. They kept together. The only literature they had was Ken's little volume containing the New Testament and the Psalms. Every man in the party read through the entire book five times. Ken lived on Psalm 116. They prayed together. They felt they were existing in the hand of God.

Finally they decided to split the party. Ken and one of his companions kept together. They learned later that their co-pilot was killed and the navigator recaptured. What happened to the rest Ken never knew.

Finally Ken made it back to the American lines. But the most remarkable thing of all was the state of his mind and body. He was neither nervous nor tired nor ill. He had never felt better. He was perfectly calm. He himself described his condition as a deep, inner spiritual peace.

There was no doubt in Ken's mind as to the source of his peace. He felt that he had committed himself without fear to the power of God. If God willed he should live, no power on earth could destroy him, but if otherwise, why, he was still in the hand of God and all was well.

In civilian life, a young business woman related this incident:

"A few days ago, on a drab winter morning, I took a taxi for the office where I work. After we had driven a short distance the driver leaned back and, speaking through the corner of his mouth, after the habit of New York cabbies, said: 'New York's a lousy place to live in. Everybody is at everybody else's throat. People's nerves are on edge. It's confusion worse confounded. A man is crazy to stay in this city if he has any chance to get away.' "

The young woman smiled and said, "I don't blame you for feeling that way. I used to feel exactly that way myself."

"Don't you feel that way now?" asked the driver. Then, looking back at his passenger, he mumbled, "You don't look like a person that would have religion. Why don't you feel that way now?"

The young lady answered, "I don't know whether you

would call it religion or not, but I have a peace deep down inside me, which I didn't have before."

"Where did that come from?" he asked.

"Every day I read my Bible," she said, "and I keep on reading until I come to a verse that I feel is God's marching orders for the day. Usually I write this down on a slip of paper and carry it with me. It keeps me steady, whatever happens."

"Did you get a verse today?" asked the driver, with heightening interest.

"Yes, I did," she answered, "and I have it here, only it begins to look as if this verse were intended for you instead of for me. You have been talking about New York as a place where confusion is worse confounded. Well, listen to what this says."

Opening her handbag, she took out a slip of paper and read these words, " 'For God is not the author of confusion but of peace.' "

"Let me see that thing," said the taxi driver, reaching back. She passed him the slip of paper and when he stopped for a red light he read it intently. Then he passed it back without a word of comment. They drove the rest of the journey in silence.

As she was leaving the taxi the young woman paid the driver and then handed him a tip. Looking at her with a quiet smile on his face, he said, "Lady, I couldn't take any tip from you. What you gave me this morning is worth more than any tips I can earn today."

On another occasion a young man testified to the help the Bible gave him in his daily work. "Two years ago," he said, "I worked temporarily selling door-to-door. I had done no selling at all before that, and I had visions of harsh rebuffs, doors slamming in my face, and the general discourtesy that is associated with this type of job.

"I decided that my sample case and knowledge of my products were not enough. I added to my equipment this verse from Luke: 'And as ye would that men should do to you, do ye also to them likewise.'

"I decided that I would treat each prospect as I would want to be treated if I were approached by a salesman at my door. I would like the salesman to be courteous. If I were not interested I would like him to withdraw graciously. I would like him, if possible, to show a little interest in me as an individual. If I showed any interest in his product, I would like him to make his presentation as brief as possible and in a low, pleasant voice.

"I went out that fateful first day and put the Golden Rule into action as best I could. An unplanned opportunity soon presented itself. When I was invited into a house and the woman wanted to discuss something of interest to herself, I listened with genuine interest, because I *was* interested in my customers. When I was turned down I smiled and thanked the woman. I felt that she expected and merited this.

"Not every prospect I called on bought from me, by any means, but I knew I made more sales by applying the Golden Rule. At the end of my two months I discovered that the amount of my average sale was fifty per cent greater than that of the average beginning salesman in that line. I had proved the value of my spiritual sales aid."

Chapter 2

The Dateless Wonder

AT FIRST glance, the Bible seems like strange reading matter in our high-powered age. Its place-names sound peculiar: Samaria, Kirjath-jearim, Beer-sheba, Galilee, Ashdod, Cana, Jericho. Its characters answer to unusual names: Isaiah, Habakkuk, Nahum, Magdalene, Tabitha. Its heroes fought with strange weapons, ate unfamiliar foods, played instruments whose sounds we cannot imagine and apparently used strange, crude turns of speech.

At first glance the Bible looks as old-fashioned as its detractors claim it is.

But the odd thing about the Bible is this: although seemingly bogged down in its tales of moldy kings, time-encrusted wars and crumbled cities, its heart still beats as strongly as ever! Underneath its antiquated exterior, truth is waiting to be laid bare.

For the Bible enjoys perennial youth. Time cannot wither it, nor antiquity age it. What it says is still as relevant as when the words were first recorded. Although its writers had no idea that it would speak to all times, all men, in all lands and in virtually all languages, *it nevertheless has*. If you put certain radioactive elements into a stew, the scientists tell us, it will keep boiling for aeons. And so with the Bible. It is as much alive in the twentieth century as it was in the fifth. It is as relevant in a scientific age as in the ancient pastoral settings from which it emerged.

One day recently a skeptical chief of an African village was listening to a missionary read one of Paul's letters from the Bible. When the missionary had finished the chief asked, "When did you say that was written?"

"About nineteen hundred years ago," replied the missionary.

"Now I know you are a liar," exclaimed the chief. "That was written about our village!"

Another story concerns the eighteenth-century French philosopher, Voltaire. He once remarked that within a hundred years the Bible would be a forgotten book, found only in museums and read only by scholars. When the hundred years were up, Voltaire's home in Geneva was occupied by the Geneva Bible Society.

The reason for the Bible's vitality, of course, is the unchanging nature of man. The outward trappings of society may change, from fighting with spears to fighting with bombs, but the urges in man do not change. Once you have learned to sift the eternal truth of the Bible's statements from the details of its outward events you will find a new source of strength in your life. The purpose of the present volume is to help you penetrate the outer difficulties of the Bible (and no one will deny that they are many) and enter the main stream of its ageless teachings.

An interesting sidelight on the timelessness of the Bible was brought up recently in the modern state of Israel. Besides being timeless spiritually, the Bible in some ways is very up-to-date geologically.

About twenty years ago a biblical archaeologist puzzled over this passage in the book of I Kings: "All these vessels, which Hiram made to King Solomon for the house of the

Lord, were of bright brass. In the plain of Jordan did the king cast them in the clay ground." The archaeologist knew the word brass meant copper. But if these mines ever existed they had disappeared for almost three thousand years. Following the Bible's directions, he came upon a site which local Arabs said their ancestors called Copper Ruin. He excavated, and found many crumbled walls and furnaces black with heaps of copper slag. Pottery in all of them was from the time of King Solomon. Here, at last, were King Solomon's famous mines!

Today the area is a hubbub of activity. "Wherever we find the richest outcroppings," the chief mining engineer said, "we come upon the slag and furnaces of Solomon's miners. We often get the feeling that someone has just left."

An industrialist began his search for oil through a study of the Bible. He read in Genesis, "Then the Lord rained upon Sodom and upon Gomorrah brimstone and fire from the Lord out of heaven; . . . and lo, the smoke of the country went up as the smoke of a furnace." To the industrialist these rising flames meant natural gas, which indicates the presence of oil. Geologists found evidence of oil, and Israel's first well was drilled in November, 1953.

It is not necessary to be a scholar to understand the Bible. But you do have to know something about when and how it came to be written, what were the concerns of its writers and something of the literary methods they used to convey their message. Once you know these things, even sketchily, you will be able to say with Samuel Coleridge, the English poet, "It finds me." And with Sir Walter Scott, sitting in his arm chair in his library at Abbotsford, "There is no other book now; it is the Bible." You will know what Lincoln mean when he said, "Keep your Bible open and you will not find the door of heaven shut."

What, exactly, does the Bible say about the questions which have haunted men since the beginning of time and which cling so tenaciously to life today? Does the Bible resolve them? Can it penetrate into these shadows? Such questions go to the very heart of the issue we present in this book.

First: The Bible Introduces You to God

There is in the heart of every man a timeless, indefinable yearning for something without which he can never know peace, joy or strength. Underneath this topsy-turvy world there is the longing for something that will give stability to life. We have a way of saying that this is a new world and that new forces are at work; but in many ways this is the same old world it has always been.

When you bring your longing for stability to the Bible, you find it helps you with your quest. You meet people who have asked themselves the same questions about the universe, long before you, and have come up with answers that satisfied them thoroughly. As you read, a strange thing happens to you. Little by little you discover that their answers have the power to satisfy you too. Words you read in the book of Psalms now seem to speak not just for the writer but for you yourself: "My soul waiteth for the Lord more than they that watch for the morning"; "The Lord is my light and my salvation;" "Lead me to the rock that is higher than I."

You meet this same questing for God and soul-satisfying answers in the book of Job. It is the story of a man who, stripped of his possessions, his family and his health, cries out in the night for someone who can tell him why an upright man like himself must suffer. Through the long night of pain, misunderstanding and adversity, Job comes to acknowl-

edge a wisdom and presence superior to his own and so find
the comfort and peace that had always eluded him before.

The Bible is primarily a book about God. It is not a book
about science although it contains much scientific data. It
is not a book about botany although it has some lovely things
to say about flowers. It is not a book on astronomy although
it tells us about the stars. It is not a book of jurisprudence
although law is there. It is not pure history although the
excitement of great events moves across its pages.

The Bible is primarily the work of writers who were concerned with unveiling God to their fellow men. It is full of
fine poetry, stirring drama, romance and intriguing biography: but all these are secondary to its central preoccupation. At the heart of the Bible is a record of God's presence.
"If with all your hearts ye truly seek me, ye shall surely find
me, thus saith our God," the Bible says at one point. The
book's purpose is to help you find God.

Perhaps you know the story of the child Samuel. He was
to grow up into one of Israel's foremost prophets, a man
whose authority and insight gave him the power to make and
unmake the first of Israel's kings. Three times one night
while the child Samuel was asleep in the Temple he heard
a voice calling him. Three times he rose from his couch in
answer to the voice and ran to the aged priest Eli to ask why
he had called him. Twice Eli denied that he had called him.
But when Samuel appeared the third time Eli knew whose
voice it was that the lad had been hearing.

"Go, lie down," he told Samuel, "and it shall be, if he call
thee, that thou shalt say, Speak, Lord; for Thy servant heareth."

In episodes like this, God enters upon the pages of the
Bible.

Another story that testifies to the presence of God is the

famous story of David. Hardly more than a boy, David volunteers to fight a Philistine soldier who delighted in making a laughingstock of the Hebrew army. David is smaller than Goliath, younger, a veteran of no wars. But David has felt the moral support of God in a deep personal way that cannot be denied.

David shouts his only battle cry just before the engagement: "Thou comest to me with a sword, and with a spear, and with a shield: but I come to thee in the name of the Lord of hosts, the God of the armies of Israel, whom thou hast defied. This day will the Lord deliver thee into mine hand."

When you ask, therefore, what is the Bible's basic purpose, the answer is clear: it is to introduce you to a God who lives. The men and women of the Bible are possessed by the thought of God; their testimony constitutes the secret of the book's inspiration.

Second: The Bible Makes You Feel Important

Perhaps there is no mood as real today as the feeling of insignificance. Many people have convinced themselves that they do not count; they are sure the world has passed them by. Great movements are surging through the world, but they will never have a chance to share in them. It doesn't matter whether they gain or lose, live or die; they have made themselves prisoners of defeat.

Clarence Darrow, the famous trial lawyer, once said: "I will give you my definition of life: life is an unpleasant interruption of nothingness."

Many have come to that conclusion: life has no meaning, it offers nothing to live for. Their personalities never come to focus on some great task or commitment.

Now turn to the Bible and notice how its message penetrates that darkness. Page after page is aflame with the story of what men can make of their lives.

The Bible teaches by telling the stories of people. It is always saying, "Look what you can do with life if you only have stamina and courage." Moses may think himself inadequate for the responsibilities which are piled on him, but when he places his hands in the hand of God he becomes one of the great men of history and the founder of the earth's most enduring people. Amos, only a herdsman in the mountaintop village of Tekoa, finds the courage to descend like a whirlwind on the corrupt, luxurious city and tongue-lash its smug citizens because they have forgotten justice and mercy. In the Bible a fallen woman by the well becomes a city missionary; a slave girl becomes the instrument through which a general is cleansed of leprosy; a vicious, intolerant bigot becomes a preacher of the universal gospel of love.

Again and again we find that the stone which the builders rejected has become the headstone of the corner. Nothing can keep these people down. To read about the odds they faced and overcame is a tonic to any soul. The Bible inspires you because of the inspiring characters that march in almost unbroken procession through its pages.

Third: The Bible Helps You Find Forgiveness

What has the Bible to say in a lonely world haunted by a sense of guilt and seeking forgiveness? The Bible lights up the darkness by assuring us that judgment never speaks the last word. The Bible gives us amazing resources for redemption. It can make the drunkard sober, the miser magnanimous and the sinner a saint. To an age overwhelmed with regret and transgression comes its gospel of redeeming grace.

When Evangeline Booth of the Salvation Army was on a world tour, she visited a little village in India where lived the families and members of the robber caste. The village was full of thieves and thugs. Every attempt by the government to stamp out the wrong had failed. Then the government resolved to destroy the village entirely and scatter the people.

The Salvation Army asked if it could have a chance to do something to save the village before the decree was carried out. The request was granted. A little band of Salvationists preached along the roadside and in the rice fields. Before long the chief of the caste was converted and finally the entire village population had been baptized. Strangely enough, stealing stopped; not a complaint was made against its people. The village had been completely transformed.

The government police thought this was too good to last and, sure enough, the robbers were seen visiting the next village. Thinking another robbery was afoot, the police sent secret agents to shadow their leader. Late one evening they saw him slinking down a narrow trail with something under his arm wrapped in newspaper. They followed him to his home, then watched through the window as he entered, closed the door, gathered his family about him and unwrapped the bundle. Loot? No. To their surprise they saw that the bundle contained a Bible which they learned later he had borrowed from a friend in the next village. The children gathered about him near the light, and through the open window they heard a clear voice reading, "Though your sins be as scarlet, they shall be as white as snow; though they be red like crimson, they shall be as wool."

The Bible had offered its redemption to this family and this village.

Dr. Joseph Sizoo tells this story: "Some years ago, early in my ministry, I came to know and to befriend a man who was later convicted of murder. I stayed with him through his long trial and his imprisonment in Sing Sing. I visited him often in the death house. One day I asked the guard who was always with me when I talked with the prisoner, if I could give him a copy of the New Testament. The guard looked the book over very carefully and handed it to the condemned man through the steel screen which separated us.

"I well remember the visit I had with him a week later. It was his last night on earth. As I walked through the corridor with the guard, he heard us coming, and walking to the door of his steel cage said to me, 'That man Luke wrote a great story.' His face was lit up with a light and a peace that I had never seen before. Of course it would be Luke who, of all gospel writers, stresses redemption for those who have lost their way, for sheep that are lost, for lilies that fade and for prodigals who step across the pathway of indiscretion."

The parable of the prodigal son has been called the greatest story ever told. It was told by Jesus, and in the King James Version of the Bible consists of just three hundred and twenty-one words, of which all but sixty-three are words of one syllable. It can be read in two minutes. It is reprinted here to show you how clearly and completely the Bible speaks in this brief tale.

It is a story told by Jesus to illustrate the unchanging fatherhood of God, and his constant readiness to forgive. For even when the wayward son returns he is still precious in his father's eyes, just as all men, however lost, are precious in the eyes of God.

A certain man had two sons: and the younger of them said to his father, "Father, give me the portion of goods that falleth to me." And he divided unto them his living. And not many days after the younger son gathered all together, and took his journey into a far country, and there wasted his substance with riotous living. And when he had spent all, there arose a mighty famine in that land; and he began to be in want. And he went and joined himself to a citizen of that country; and he sent him into his fields to feed swine. And he would fain have filled his belly with the husks that the swine did eat: and no man gave unto him.

And when he came to himself, he said, "How many hired servants of my father's have bread enough and to spare, and I perish with hunger! I will arise and go to my father, and will say unto him, 'Father, I have sinned against heaven, and before thee, and am no more worthy to be called thy son: make me as one of thy hired servants.' "

And he arose, and came to his father. But when he was yet a great way off, his father saw him, and had compassion, and ran, and fell on his neck, and kissed him. And the son said unto him, "Father, I have sinned against heaven, and in thy sight, and am no more worthy to be called thy son."

But the father said to his servants, "Bring forth the best robe, and put it on him; and put a ring on his hand, and shoes on his feet: and bring hither the fatted calf, and kill it; and let us eat, and be merry: for this my son was dead, and is alive again; he was lost and is found." And they began to be merry.

Now his elder son was in the field: and as he came and drew nigh to the house, he heard musick and dancing. And he called one of the servants, and asked what these things meant. And he said unto him, "Thy brother is come; and thy father hath killed the fatted calf, because he hath received him safe and sound." And he was angry, and would not go in: therefore came his father out and intreated him. And he answering said to his father, "Lo, these many years do I serve thee, neither transgressed I at any time thy commandment: and yet thou never gavest me a kid, that I might make merry with my friends: but as soon as this thy son was come, which hath devoured thy living with harlots, thou hast killed for him the fatted calf." And he said unto him, "Son, thou art ever with me, and all that I have is thine. It was meet that we should make merry and be glad: for this thy brother was dead, and is alive again; and was lost, and is found."

Fourth: The Bible Holds Out Hope

There is no more dramatic story in the Bible than the one in the fourteenth chapter of the book of Exodus. Moses has led his people one day's journey out of Egypt. Hungry and weary, they have pitched their camp somewhere along the shores of the Red Sea. As they wonder how to get across this barrier, they turn and see a cloud of dust arising against the setting sun behind them. To their horror, they recognize in the distance the horses and chariots of Pharaoh's army in hot pursuit.

They turn furiously on Moses for having led them into this tragic trap. There they are, the trackless dunes of the desert on either side, the sea in front of them and Pharaoh driving furiously upon them from the rear.

At that moment Moses turns to God. Above the rattle of the chariots and the tumult of the panic-stricken people, Moses hears God say: "Speak to the children of Israel that they go forward." And the rest of the story you know. Or do you? If not, look it up in the fourteenth chapter of Exodus. After you have finished it, take another three minutes to read the next chapter too, where it is retold in lines of breathless poetry.

The story of Moses is just one chapter in the Bible's message of hope and deliverance. This victorious message binds the book into a single living whole and gives it the ring of finality and triumph. The Bible assures us that history has a purpose, that truth prevails, and that the mighty issues of goodness and truth may be deferred and postponed but never defeated.

We think of Paul as the great apostle who carried the new religion beyond the little land where it was born. We think of him as one of the big figures of his day and generation. Judging him by his influence upon the centuries, this is so.

But not when he was living. When he tried to talk to the people of Athens, they shrugged their shoulders and walked away. To the people of Ephesus and Corinth and Philippi, big metropolitan cities of his day, he was just another eccentric babbler trying to get a hearing. In our city parks today we often come across odd, fanatical speakers who strike us just as Paul must have appeared to the people of his day. But Paul was not shaken by his contemporaries' scorn of him. He was undiscourageable. The book of The Acts of The Apostles tells of his trials, his persistence, and his ultimate triumph. It is the testimony of a man who would not stay down.

Have you ever heard an older person say, "Thank God I am old and I won't have to live in this mess much longer?" Perhaps you have. To many of us, young and old alike, life is a squirrel cage going round and round, but getting nowhere. By contrast, so many of the people of the New Testament faced life undiscouraged, unashamed and unafraid. The word "problem," which we toss so glibly off our lips, you will find nowhere in the New Testament. Nor must we think they had no problems in those days. In the midst of the power and grandeur of the Roman Empire, what was the early Christian church? A mere handful of unimpressive people meeting under cover of night in some upper room or other secret place, and singing and talking about a leader who had been executed as a felon in a remote Jewish city. How ridiculous, on the surface of it, for them to think they could make a dent upon their world.

And yet their Roman neighbors, later watching them in action, cried with dismay that they were turning the world upside down!

The reason for their zeal? Their faith and hope had made them spiritual giants. They were convinced that truth is more powerful than falsehood, that sharing is more divine than saving, and that giving is more blessed than getting. They knew that in this world Pontius Pilate never has the last word.

Maybe you have tried to surmount some obstacle and failed. Maybe your children seem unappreciative at times, even wayward. Maybe your health is poor or your job is petering out. And if you are the kind that keeps your troubles to yourself, you find your discouragement becoming deeper with life growing darker as the days go by.

Has it ever occurred to you that the Bible can be useful in times like these? You had heard the preacher read it at a funeral service of a friend, but it seemed just a formal bit of ceremony then. Now is the time to read it to yourself. Put your own name in the places where the text reads "you" or "a man." Throw your imagination into gear. Maybe you have forgotten you had an imagination.

If you thumb through the book of Psalms, one psalm may seem to leap from the page and speak directly to you. Here is part of Psalm 121, certainly one of the most comforting poems ever written:

> The Lord is thy keeper:
> The Lord is thy shade upon thy right hand.
> The sun shall not smite thee by day,
> Nor the moon by night.
> The Lord shall preserve thee from all evil:
> He shall preserve thy soul.
> The Lord shall preserve thy going out and thy coming in
> From this time forth, and even for evermore.

Or you may want to read some of the matchless promises of the prophets, those great men who felt that God spoke directly to them. Here is part of the sixtieth chapter of Isaiah:

The sun shall be no more thy light by day;
Neither for brightness shall the moon give light unto thee:
But the Lord shall be unto thee an everlasting light,
And thy God thy glory.
Thy sun shall no more go down;
Neither shall thy moon withdraw itself:
For the Lord shall be thine everlasting light,
And the days of thy mourning shall be ended.

There is an old fable that tells how the devil once thought of going out of business and held an auction to dispose of his tools. Malice, hatred, envy, greed—they were all put up for sale and sold. But the devil had placed one tool off by itself with the highest price tag of all. It was called "discouragement." It had been priced so high because it was the most valuable. When all other tools had failed, this one could be used to pry open a man, get inside him and destroy him.

The Bible is the world's most tested cure for discouragement. Let us close this chapter with one more story of its powers.

The service on the dining car had been very unsatisfactory. Seven times the four travelers had asked for a glass of water before it was served; the salad never arrived. There was every reason to complain but the four men took it good naturedly. When the waiter brought the dessert he said, "I want to apologize for my service this evening."

He was assured it was all right, since the men thought he was new at this job and they knew it took considerable experience to serve acceptably on a dining car.

But the waiter said, "No, I'm not new. I have served for years. But as the train left Harrisburg I got a wire from my wife telling me our little girl was killed by an auto on the street and I'm kind of nervous."

When asked why he had continued the trip, he replied,

"We were short two men and I couldn't do Marjorie any good; and I felt it was my duty to carry on."

One of the men was a Secretary of the American Bible Society. He took from his pocket a copy of the gospel of John offering it to the bereaved man. But the waiter put up his hand. "I know that book," he said. "It's the only thing that keeps me going tonight. Thank you very much anyway."

Chapter 3

Other Glories of the Book

THE GREATEST glory of the Bible is its power to *change* men's lives. The books of the world with even a little of this power can be counted on the fingers of one hand. Many books contain fine prose-writing, drama, keen analysis, breath-taking scientific revelation—but the Bible reaches out to the heart and conscience of man.

In the previous two chapters we have tried to make clear this living power of the Bible. We have tried to show that the book is not a dumb, inert mass of paper and ink (though every copy not opened and read is just that) or a faint echo of a distant past. One more illustration would not be out of place; it is perhaps the most moving of all.

When the Japanese were on a spy hunt in Burma, anyone who could read was suspect and it was almost a crime to be found in possession of a book. But books were precious and people took to hiding them. Some Christians hid their prayer books and Testaments in the pillow they used at night, others wrapped them in waterproof leaves from palm trees and hid them in the forest.

But a few were too proud of their faith to conceal it. One man left his New Testament openly in his house. Finally, the inevitable happened. A Japanese soldier discovered it. Pointing his bayonet at the man, the soldier asked, "What is this book?"

Never flinching, the Christian replied, "That is my Bible,

43

my life. Where I go it must go with me, and without it I should die."

There was a long pause while the two men looked into each other's eyes. Then the soldier lowered his bayonet, turned around and left the hut. He never reported the incident nor did he ever return.

Yet the Bible has other glories besides its power to touch the mainspring of men's actions. By reading it, you reach the bedrock on which our culture is built. For Western civilization is founded on the Bible. More of our ideas, our wisdom, our literature, our music, our art come from the Bible than from all other books put together. It has shaped and influenced our world more than any other book.

William Lyon Phelps of Yale once wrote, "I thoroughly believe in a university education for both men and women; but I believe a knowledge of the Bible without a college course is more valuable than a college course without the Bible."

To prove the importance of the Bible in shaping our cultural world, let us try to imagine what it would be like to wake up and discover that the Book of Books had disappeared and all traces of its influence had vanished. Let us suppose it was as completely erased from the record of men as though it had never existed. This would be the result:

First, the great art galleries would have massive empty frames on the walls, for the artistry of the world has drawn much of its inspiration from the lost book.

Much of the world's music would be silenced. The mighty oratorios would no longer be heard, the hymns expressing the hopes and fears of human hearts would have died away. Christmas with its rejuvenating carols would be gone. There would be little great music left, for it had so drawn upon the lost book that whole pages were now missing.

The libraries would look as if billions of moths had descended on the printed pages. The works of authors like Shakespeare, Dante, Milton, Bunyan, Tennyson, Tolstoy, Dostoyevsky and hundreds of others, would be often unintelligible, because of the many omissions. The volumes of oratory of the last two thousand years would be without their highest flights. The law books would no longer make sense for their fundamental principles would be eliminated.

The Magna Carta of Britain, the Constitution of the United States, the Declaration of Independence, the Bill of Rights and all great statements of liberty would be practically wiped blank, except for a few commonplace words.

Wherever the English language was spoken, men would stammer and be unable to express themselves, for the lost book had fashioned their native tongue. And not only would this be true in English-speaking lands, but in other countries as well, for the Bible in the native tongue had always helped greatly to fashion speech.

But the loss of the book would cut even deeper. Values would become blurred. Human life would grow cheap. Men would become tools to be used. Life would grow invalid and meaningless. Without the Bible, the earth would change in all but the barest essentials of life.

So much for the negative side: a world without the Bible. Now let us turn to the positive. Let us try tracing the effect of the Bible on our cultural life: our speech, our names, our literature, our music and our painting.

The early translators of the English Bible, William Tyndale and Miles Coverdale, actually combined words in such expressive ways that their combinations have since passed into daily speech. From Tyndale came new words like "peacemaker," "long-suffering," "broken-hearted," and "scapegoat." From Coverdale came "lovingkindness," "morning-star," "kindhearted," "tender mercy." The word "beautiful" was not known in literature until Tyndale used it. And through the use of the Hebrew phrase, "holy of holies," has come the characteristic form of expression we find in "heart of hearts," "place of all places" and "evil of evils."

However, it is the later King James or Authorized Version of 1611 whose prose has lingered longest in the ears of all English-speaking peoples. Countless of its phrases are used so often, sound so familiar, that the user only dimly knows, if at all, that they come from the Bible—"apple of his eye," "clear as crystal," "fat of the land," "handwriting on the wall," "labor of love," "powers that be," "salt of the earth," "a good old age," "a drop in the bucket," "the signs of the times," "a thorn in the flesh," "a crown of life," "all things to all men," "the skin of my teeth," "a man after his own heart," "in the twinkling of an eye," "filthy lucre," "to eat, drink and be merry," "at the parting of the way," and "the wings of the morning."

More than its phrases, the great people and events of the Bible have come to serve as a sort of conversational shorthand, enabling us to imply a great deal by saying little. We speak of someone as "a good Samaritan," and conjure up the image of a man who goes far out of his way to help others. We speak of "a doubting Thomas" as a man who questions a basic tenet, just as the apostle Thomas questioned Jesus' resurrection. We refer to a Judas, a Methuselah, the wisdom of Solomon, the patience of Job, the strength of Samson. Other characters have other meanings—Lazarus, Daniel, Jezebel. And names of the books of the Bible became useful: an exodus can now refer to any departure, although in the Bible it refers only to Israel's departure from Egypt. The word "gospel," which originally meant only "good news," has come in our day to mean "genuine," as in "gospel truth."

Jeremiah, the sorrowing prophet, gave his name to the English word "jeremiad."

Bible men and women have given their names to each living generation in an unending stream. The name "Mary" is borne by about six million American women today. From it have developed no less than sixty-five other women's names, beginning with Marie, Marian, Marilyn, Marianne and Marsha.

Following Mary, we have the man's name "John." One American man in twelve is now named John and there are ninety-three additional names derived from it. As for last names, America now has more than a million Johnsons, two thirds of a million Joneses, and countless families that go by the name of Jackson, Jennings, Jenks, Evans, Hanson and Hancock. These are all derivations of the name John, the last two through the Hans in the German equivalent for John—Johannes.

Two thirds of all United States Presidents had one or more Bible names.

America is peppered with names of cities and sites drawn from the Bible. An amusing story about this is told concerning the mayors of the twin cities, St. Paul and Minneapolis, who often teased each other about the relative merits of their two cities. At a banquet, the mayor of St. Paul arose and said, "Gentlemen, I leave it up to you. Look in the Bible, the rock-bottom source of truth, and count the number of mentions of Minneapolis as against those of St. Paul."

The Puritans, although founding their community on the Bible, limited themselves to naming two places after it: Salem and Sharon in Massachusetts. However, over the years, Americans have dubbed eleven "Beulahs," nine "Canaans," eleven "Jordans," and twenty more "Sharons." The pious German sects who settled eastern Pennsylvania used their Bible in naming Ephrata, Nazareth, Emmaus and Bethlehem.

The Bible has proved a boon to authors in search of an eye-catching title for their books, novels and plays. At least two thousand contemporary books bear titles with a biblical allusion. To name just a few, *Generation of Vipers, East of Eden, My Son, My Son!, The Years of the Locust, The Least of These, The Angel with the Trumpet, The Seven Pillars of Wisdom.*

A recent study of the New York *Times* editorial page revealed 466 biblical verses, phrases and references in 367 editorials appearing in 262 days. Charles A. Dana, one of America's great journalists, once said to some students about the Bible, "I am considering it now not as a religious book, but as a manual of utility, of professional preparation and professional use for a journalist. There is perhaps no book whose style is more suggestive and instructive."

On another occasion, Dana was having trouble with a reporter who was told to cover a news event in a thousand words. The reporter insisted on being allowed fifteen hundred words. This is what Dana wired back: *"One Thousand. Moses Covered the Creation in 864."*

Allusions to Bible events and characters permeate the world's literature. Shakespeare is full of them; Chaucer, Milton, Dickens, Yeats, Melville, Hardy, Carlyle, George Eliot, Thoreau, yield far more of their meaning when you understand their allusions to the Bible. In fact, the narrator of Melville's *Moby Dick* is symbolically called Ishmael, after the outcast son of Abraham, and the whole novel opens with the simple, meaningful sentence, "Call me Ishmael."

Knowing your Bible can help you with all your reading. It can illuminate passages that you once had to skip over. Since the Bible has been a source of more simile, metaphor and allusion than any other book in the world, familiarity with it will clarify many an author's words. In Shakespeare's *Henry IV*, for example, we find this jibe, "He surely knows by experience the story of the prodigal." To the Bible reader this conjures up the image of an inheritance wasted in riotous living, while to the person without the same knowledge, it is only another obscurity in Shakespeare.

Shakespeare knew his Bible thoroughly. There are verbal and historical inaccuracies in his references, for he doubtless depended on memory in his prolific production, but the many references and quotations prove that the Bible was deeply woven into his thought. There are about twelve hundred of these references and quotes, including 149 passages from Matthew, 138 from Psalms, 64 from Genesis and 42 from Job.

But aside from the literal use of the Bible in names of people and places, in turns of everyday speech, in book titles and as quotations and figures of speech in literary works, there is a deeper stream of biblical influence running through our lives. The Bible has shaped the style and vocabulary of all people who have spoken and written English for almost three centuries.

This can be traced back to the state of the English language when the Bible appeared in its greatest and most popular translation, the King James Version of 1611. English was still in a formative stage then, still fresh and expanding. It had not yet hardened into a permanent form. In those days, the Bible was a household book. Virtually every family read, studied and pondered it. Its forms of expression worked themselves into the popular subconscious mind and actually helped form the character of English as we speak it today.

How shall we analyze the Bible's language? First, it is simple and direct. Second, it is rhythmic. Third, it is lucid. These three qualities: directness, rhythm and lucidity, are typical of good English as it is spoken today. They are echoes of the diction found in the Bible. Whether we are conscious of it or not, the Bible's way of putting things has penetrated our language and helped make English the powerful, flexible language it is.

The process of remolding the English language along these lines was helped by the Bible's popularity with great writers of English. It became the touchstone of English style, and all English writers have used its vocabulary whether they were swayed by its teachings or not.

Edward Gibbon in his *Decline and Fall of the Roman Empire,* wrote prose that has long been considered a model of stateliness. But its flow, its long rise and ebb, are a direct reflection of the style of the King James Version. The work of Francis Bacon mirrors another facet of the Bible's style: its short, crisp sentences, which Bacon imitated, adding his own ornamentation. Milton, besides using biblical themes, as in his *Paradise Lost* and *Paradise Regained,* kept the rolling scriptural rhythms in both his prose and poetry. The loose flow of Walt Whitman's poetry, often regarded as something quite new in American letters, was a style used centuries ago by the Hebrew prophets—all of whom rejected rhyme and strict rhythms and insisted on complete freedom of form for their thoughts.

Hawthorne, Emerson and Thoreau all have a biblical strain in their writings. In fact Thoreau, harsh and denunciatory but tender at heart, has been called "the Jeremiah of the Western world." Emerson called the Bible "the most original book in the world," "the alphabet of the nations," and "an engine of education of the first power."

But let the great writers of the world speak for themselves on the Bible as a source of literary inspiration. Coleridge said, "A study of the Bible will keep any man from being vulgar in style." Ruskin wrote that his taste was due to learning by heart certain chapters of the Bible. A noted orator asked Charles Dickens for the most pathetic story in literature; the answer was the Prodigal Son. Another asked Daniel Webster for the greatest legal digest and got the answer—the Sermon on the Mount. Milton gave to the Psalms and the Prophets first place in all the literature of the world. Jonathan Swift, the satirist who gave us *Gulliver's Travels,* said, "The translators of our Bible were masters of an English style much fitter for that work than any which we see in our present writings, which I take to be owing to the simplicity that runs through the whole."

To be born into the English language is automatically to fall heir to the glories of the English Bible. The book has come far since its beginning. Written in the East in original words that few can understand, it has leaped over the barriers of language, time and place. It has influenced the speaking habits of millions. It has influenced the writing habits of men who disagreed with it. In fact, the Bible has fulfilled its own prophecy, "Their line is gone out through all the earth, and their words to the end of the world."

The thought of the Bible's effect on music is likely to bring the name of George Friedrich Handel to mind. Although he was born in Germany, Handel spent the last half of his life in England. Handel wrote seventeen oratorios on subjects taken from the Bible—among them *Saul, Samson, Israel in Egypt* and *Joseph.* In his crowning work, *The Messiah,* Handel set to music certain passages from the book of Isaiah, the Gospels, the Psalter and the book of Revelation. Handel is quoted as having said that during the composition of the *Hallelujah Chorus,* "I did think I did see all Heaven before me, and the great God himself."

American Negro spirituals are probably the most direct expression of the Bible in our music. They show how the slaves felt about the great moments in the Bible. They are

vivid and completely personal, with a directness that the religious poetry of the white races has rarely equalled. Consider some of the titles: "Were You There When They
Crucified My Lord?", "The Old Ark's Er Movin'," and "O,
Didn't It Rain!", about the flood; "Wrestlin' Jacob," the
story of Jacob wrestling with the angel. The Bible's story of
the Resurrection is recorded in "Where Shall I Be When the
First Trumpet Sounds?" and also, "The Great Getting-up
Day." When the slaves identified themselves with the captive
children of Israel in Egypt, they found expression in such
great songs as "Go Down, Moses," and "Deep River."

Some spirituals mention several biblical events. In "He
Is Just the Same Today," we find mention of Moses crossing
the Red Sea, Daniel in the lion's den, and David and Goliath. In "Wasn't That a Mornin'?" we hear about Samson
slaying the Philistines, Adam and Eve, and the story of Nico-
demus.

Of course, the Bible has found great expression in the
music of the Church, to the extent that chants, litanies and
hymns draw on its message. The cantatas of Bach draw much
of their inspiration from the Bible, and Mendelssohn in his
oratorio, *Elijah,* tells in music the story of that stern and
solitary prophet.

The influence of the Bible on painting needs little elab-
oration here. For the layman, it is hard to think of more
than a handful of paintings acknowledged to be masterpieces
that do not draw on the Bible for their subjects. Imagine
how impoverished the art of the world would be without Da
Vinci's "Last Supper," Michelangelo's Sistine Chapel frescoes, Raphael's Madonnas, without the countless scenes from
the Gospels portrayed by El Greco, Titian, Rubens, Van
Dyke, Velázquez, Dürer, Rembrandt and others. Knowing
the Bible also enriches our perception of these paintings. For
example, Rubens' canvas showing Susanna and the Elders

yields double the meaning if you know the story behind the events. All the figures take on a new dimension in your imagination. Too many people fail to enjoy some of the world's treasures simply because they do not know their Bible.

But what of religion itself? What information does the Bible offer on religion?

All of the Bible is holy to Christians and the Old Testament is holy to Jews. To members of either religion, the Bible is the one unimpeachable source of information about the birth and early days of their faith. It is the fountainhead of all their beliefs and customs. In the Bible we discover the record of the events that have been celebrated for thousands of years.

The best way to renew your acquaintance with the basic tenets of your religion is to read about them first-hand in the Bible. Just as no one ever learned to play a musical instrument by watching someone else play, so the best way to learn about religion is from its truest source.

You will find all the great events of the church calendar glowingly described in the Bible: Epiphany, Palm Sunday, Holy Week, Easter, Ascension Day, Pentecost, Advent, Christmas, not to mention the round of Jewish feasts. And the first telling of these events is always the best. No digests you have read, or sermons based on them, no picture-stories showing them, can compare with their first breathless telling in the Bible. Hollywood's gorgeous epics, for all the fortunes spent on them, cannot compare in narrative power with some pages of the Bible. The closing chapters of the gospel of Mark, describing the last days of Jesus' earthly life have a starkness and drama which make most writing seem trivial by comparison.

Why not try reading them soon? Why not tonight?

Chapter 4

The Most Exciting Book
in the World

THE BIBLE has not swayed the world simply because of its great themes. Suppose they had been treated, as they have by many writers, in heavy philosophical lingo? Would the Bible still hold its high place? Probably not.

As someone has said, the message is not argued out; it is acted out. The Bible talks about people, not ideal people, but real people, whose passions and virtues, loyalties and frivolities, keep them always alive. It is without exaggeration the most exciting book in the world.

Lincoln Steffens, the famous reporter and "muck-raker" had an interesting experience with the Bible. Here is what he wrote about reading the New Testament:

"What did the Christians believe, exactly? I decided then and there to read the New Testament the next time I was at home and had time, not myself to believe, but to see what the good church-going Christians believed.

"The experience was an adventure so startling that I wanted everybody else to have it; I still recommend people to read the New Testament as I read it, without reverence, with feet up on the desk and a pipe in the mouth, as news. It *is* news. It made the stuff I was writing in the magazine, old stuff. All my stories of all the cities and states were one story . . . and these were all in that old story of Christ in the New Testament."

The truth is that the Bible makes wonderful reading—*just* as reading. There is writing to everybody's taste, and there should be, because among its authors there was a shepherd, a doctor, a king, a farmer, a historian, a poet, a fisherman, a priest, a lawyer and a philosopher—and that does not exhaust the list. For the most part they wrote independently of one another, over a period of two thousand years. You have in the Bible twenty centuries of changing life.

A Gallup poll recently revealed that the American people consider the Bible "the most interesting" book they had ever read. And this was a choice over the detective, historical and sex-laden story-telling of our times.

The test of a good story is whether you want to read it again. That is what gives long life to books. Dickens and Shakespeare have endured for this reason. Once you have sampled parts of your Bible, you will find yourself turning and returning to them. You will come to feel that no poem can match the haunting loveliness of the Twenty-third Psalm, that no love story can touch you like the tale of Ruth, no moral teaching like the Sermon on the Mount. You will feel that no heroine ever had the courage of Esther, or the purity of Susanna. You will be sure that no history-writing matches The Acts for excitement.

In a recent poll in England, people were asked to indicate which of these books they owned: a Bible, a cookbook, a dictionary, a book on gardening. The Bible outstripped all others by ninety per cent. In Brazil, over a million copies of scripture were distributed in 1954. In Japan, after World War II, the Bible—particularly the New Testament—became the nation's best-seller. For at least three years the New Testament outsold every other book in Japan by a ratio of five to one; and this in spite of the fact that it was written in traditional Japanese rather than the everyday language used in newspapers and magazines.

What is *in* the Bible? A little girl, when asked this question by her Sunday school teacher, replied, "A lot of dates of weddings, deaths and births, some newspaper clippings, a lock of hair, some snapshots and two valentines." Our answer will take us a little farther than that.

The word "bible" is a perfect key to the actual nature of the books. It comes from the Greek "biblia," meaning books. The Bible is just that: although bound as one volume, it is really many books.

The Bible has two great divisions, the Old Testament and the New Testament. The word "testament" means a contract, a covenant, or mutual understanding, between God and his people. Each book is a record of such a contract.

The Old Testament gives us the history and religious thoughts of the ancient Jews, who were different from all other people of their time because they believed steadfastly in one God. The Old Testament opens with some of the most sonorous words ever penned, "In the beginning God created the heavens and the earth. Now the earth was without form and void, and darkness was upon the face of the deep. . . ." And ends with the vision of a day of judgment in the book of Malachi.

In between, the Old Testament records the creation of man, the early history of the world, and the founding and infancy of the Hebrew nation. It tells the stirring story of Israel's captivity in Egypt and her deliverance under Moses. It brings to life the mighty historical personalities of Samuel, Saul, David the king, his son King Solomon, and the rulers who succeeded them.

In addition to historical narratives, the Old Testament is aflame with the words of the Hebrew prophets. Also it contains a book of religious poetry known as the book of Psalms, an anthology of practical proverbs, and a number of stories, plays and philosophical writings.

The New Testament deals with the life and teachings of Jesus, and the deeds and writings of his apostles. It contains the four gospels of Matthew, Mark, Luke and John. These four narratives present, each from a different point of view, the personality and ministry of Jesus.

In the New Testament we also find a history of the early Christian church entitled The Acts of the Apostles; the letters of Paul, who devoted his life to preaching the gospel of Christ, and similar letters from other apostles.

The Old Testament is full of promises that God would give his people a deliverer. The New Testament teaches that these promises were fulfilled in the life and death of Jesus. The Old Testament contains many stories whose basic theme is faith and hope. The New Testament glows with tales of love and tolerance and redemption.

Here is a division of the books of the Bible according to their subject matter, as found in any standard Protestant Bible.

The History of the Ancient Jews

   The book of Genesis
   The book of Exodus
   The book of Leviticus
   The book of Numbers
   The book of Deuteronomy
   The book of Joshua
   The book of Judges
   The first book of Samuel
   The second book of Samuel

The first book of Kings
The second book of Kings
The first book of Chronicles
The second book of Chronicles
The book of Ezra
The book of Nehemiah

The Words of the Prophets

The book of Isaiah
The book of Jeremiah
The book of Ezekiel
The book of Hosea
The book of Joel
The book of Amos
The book of Obadiah
The book of Micah
The book of Nahum
The book of Habakkuk
The book of Zephaniah
The book of Haggai
The book of Zechariah
The book of Malachi

Poetry, Drama, Biography and Philosophy

Lamentations (poetry)
Psalms (poetry)
Song of Solomon (poetry)
Job (drama)
Ruth (biographical sketch)
Esther (biographical sketch)
Daniel (biographical sketch; also apocalyptic literature)
Jonah (biographical sketch)
Proverbs (philosophy)
Ecclesiastes (philosophy)

Biographies of Jesus

The gospel of Matthew
The gospel of Mark

The gospel of Luke
The gospel of John

A History of the Early Church

The Acts of the Apostles

The Letters of Paul

To the Romans
To the Corinthians (two letters)
To the Galatians
To the Ephesians
To the Philippians
To the Colossians
To the Thessalonians (two letters)
To Timothy (two letters)
To Titus
To Philemon

Miscellaneous Letters

To the Hebrews
The letter of James
The letters of Peter (two letters)
The letters of John (three letters)
The letter of Jude

Apocalyptic Literature

The book of Revelation

The traditional arrangement of the Bible does not carry these books in any strict order of subject matter. You find the book of Ruth, which is really a short story, placed among the historical books. You find the book of Jonah among the prophets, although it is not a book of prophecy. But it is useful to have the arrangement by subject matter firmly in mind when you begin to read the Bible.

Chapter 5

The Book Behind America

ANY AMERICAN will be encouraged in his program of Bible reading if he is familiar with the influence the book had in the origins of our own country. The beginnings of colonial life in America cannot be understood without considering the role played by the Bible.

Long before the arrival of the Pilgrims and the thousands of Puritans who followed them, the religious ideas that shaped much of our nation's attitudes had put down their roots. The fifteenth and sixteenth centuries had brought the Reformation and the invention of printing, and consequently the Bible in cheaper printed form. It was an age of few books, among which the Bible became immensely popular.

The effect of the Bible upon the England of those days was expressed by the historian John Richard Green in these words: "No greater moral change ever passed over a nation than passed over England during the years that parted the middle of the reign of Elizabeth from the meeting of the Long Parliament. England became the people of a book and that book was the Bible. The whole temper of the nation felt the change. A new conception of life and of man superseded the old. A new moral and religious impulse spread through every class."

One of the outcomes of this groundswell was the search

60

for more religious freedom which led, among other things, to the founding of American colonies. It is not surprising to find in the earliest legal code of Massachusetts, scriptural quotations on the margins to indicate the origin of the various laws. In the "Fundamental Orders of Connecticut," drawn up in 1638 we find these words, "We enter into a combination and confederation together to maintain and preserve the liberty and purity of the gospel of Our Lord Jesus Christ whom we now profess." Thus was the new-found freedom carried over to the political sphere.

The chief purpose of early American education was that the Bible might be better known. A little book called the *New England Primer* was widely used in all the colonies for more than a century before the Revolution and to some extent afterwards. It was based primarily on the Bible. In teaching children the letter "A" of the alphabet, the primer gives this rhyme:

> In Adam's fall
> We sinned all.

Beside the letter "Z" the children read:

> Zacchaeus he
> Did climb a tree
> Our Lord to see.

The same holds true of the colleges. There were ten colleges founded before the Revolution that continue to this day. Nine of them—Harvard, William and Mary, Yale, Princeton, Washington and Lee, Columbia, Brown, Rutgers and Dartmouth—opened with faculties composed of theologians whose main purpose was to train ministers of the gospel.

In early American life the Bible was regarded as one of the prime requisites of every home. When a scarcity of Bibles developed, one of the first acts of the new Congress was to authorize the printing of an American edition. When the Pony Express was started many years later, in 1860, each new rider was presented with a small leather-bound Bible by his employer. In the intervening years the book had traveled westward with the pioneers and earned a special place for itself in almost every outlying home and cabin of the growing land. Many children, isolated from schools, learned to read from their Bibles. Where all other books had been left back East, the Bible alone survived the trek across the wilderness and mountains.

Of course, the open Bible alone did not produce America's high estate of freedom. In fact, in colonial days the scriptures were often misused. It is easy for us to lampoon the Puritans for the severity with which they forced the Bible upon their children. Modern pedagogy would not tolerate the narrowness of the *New England Primer*. Nevertheless, five generations of emphasis in education upon the Bible anchored in our nation's life certain convictions that have never changed.

In the light of these facts, it is interesting to note what certain American leaders have said about the Bible.

A few months before Lincoln died, he asked his old friend, Joshua F. Speed, who had known him since the beginning of his career, to spend the night with him at the Soldiers' Home. Speed arrived early in the evening. When he entered the President's room he saw him reading a book. As Speed came nearer in the twilight he was surprised to see that it was the Bible.

"I am glad to see you so profitably engaged," he said.

"Yes," answered Lincoln, "I *am* profitably engaged."

"Well," said Speed, somewhat sadly, "if you have recovered from your skepticism, I am sorry to say that I have not."

The President looked him earnestly in his face, then placed

his hand gently on the doubter's shoulder. "You are wrong, Speed," he said. "Take all of this book on reason that you can, and the rest on faith, and you will, I am sure, live and die a happier and better man."

Earlier in Lincoln's life, when he discovered that most of the ministers of his own city of Springfield, Illinois, were against him in the presidential campaign, he was greatly disturbed. His friend, Dr. Newton Bateman, superintendent of public instruction in the state at the time, said that in a private conversation Lincoln drew a copy of the New Testament from his pocket. Bateman quoted him as saying then, "These men know that I am for freedom . . . and that my opponents are for slavery. They know this; and yet, with this book in their hands, in the light of which human bondage could not live a single moment, they are going to vote against me. I do not understand it at all. I know that there is a God and that he hates injustice and slavery . . . I know that I am right because liberty is right, for Christ teaches it . . . and these men will find that they have not read their Bible aright."

When war came, Lincoln in the White House was asked his creed. He selected this passage from the prophet Micah:

> He hath showed thee, O man, what is good;
> And what doth the Lord require of thee,
> But to do justly, and to love mercy,
> And to walk humbly with thy God?

On another occasion Lincoln said, "That the Almighty does make use of human agencies, and directly intervenes in human affairs, is one of the plainest statements in the Bible."

Woodrow Wilson was a son of the parsonage, a keen observer of America and a sound historian. Toward the end of his career he said in a speech, "I have a very simple thing to ask of you. I ask of every man and woman in this audience that, from this day on, they will realize that part of the destiny of America lies in their daily perusal of this great book."

Franklin D. Roosevelt devoted a paragraph of his last Thanksgiving Day proclamation to the matter of reading the Bible. He said, "I call upon my fellow citizens to join wholeheartedly in a nation-wide reading of the Holy Scriptures. . . . Let every man of every creed go to his own version . . . for a renewed and strengthening contact with those eternal truths and majestic principles which have inspired such measure of true greatness as this nation has achieved."

PART TWO

How to Read the Bible

Chapter 6

Digging for Gold

THERE ARE thousands of Americans who buy the Bible in order to go about the business of reading it. Knowing that it is different from other books, they may take a few precautions before starting. They may say to themselves something like this: "Well, I know brother Bill or Aunt Mary tried to read it and didn't succeed, so I think I'll adopt a plan that will *force* me to read it." So they consult the table of contents or a Bible guide, and divide the book into a set number of daily or weekly readings. They find out that if they read three chapters every day and five on Sunday, they will cover the territory in just fifty-two weeks. Or perhaps they vow to read one chapter a day. At any rate, they make themselves a tight strait jacket and grimly set about the job of reading their Bible.

Such a process would not produce much interest in any other book and it usually does not produce much in the Bible. Bible reading becomes a chore, instead of a voyage of discovery.

After the reader finds this approach does not work, he may try another. He needs guidance but finds none. After fumbling around with various approaches and suggestions, the whole business begins to seem rather unreal. Other interests crowd around; the book is closed for good.

On the following pages we have outlined a practical and

mature way to approach your Bible. Of course, it is different
from the approach to most other books, but then the Bible
is a book in a class by itself.

The first step in approaching your Bible should be taken
upstairs in the thinking department. Think of the Bible as
a tool. A tool is something that facilitates work. Some tools,
like awls or screwdrivers, cups or spoons, are simple. Others
are very complicated. Let us admit that the Bible is a complicated tool. That fact need not discourage us. Remember
that an automobile is a complicated tool also, yet millions
of people use it with the greatest of ease. We would question
the sanity of the man who did nothing but sit and admire
his new car and never learned to use it. But there is many
a man who admires his handsome copy of the Bible, and
hasn't the remotest idea how to go about using it. He doesn't
know whether the Lord's Prayer is in the Old Testament or
the New—or for that matter, even that there *is* an Old Testament and a New.

The purpose of this section is to give you your first lessons
in making use of your Bible.

The Bible can be read and studied for many purposes.
It can be read as a book of history or a book of ancient custom. It can be studied as literature. However, the most rewarding use of the Bible is its devotional use. By devotional
use, we mean religious. Both of these words are significant.
The word "devotional" comes from the same root as the word
"vow." A vow is a serious matter. It is a promise that must
be kept for honor's sake.

The word "religious" is an interesting word too. It has
the same root we find in the word "ligament." A ligament
is the tie that connects the extremities of the movable bones
in our bodies. Similarly, religion is that tie, the strongest

tie in our lives, that holds us fast to God. When you are reading the Bible in the way we are discussing it here, you are strengthening that tie.

Bible reading of this sort, which is the richest and most rewarding of all, is best begun in the spirit of prayer. It is your admission to yourself and to God that you need his help in the undertaking.

Where should you begin to read your Bible? This is probably a question you have asked yourself several times in the course of reading this book, and perhaps many times before. It is a good question. Many a man (and woman) has closed his Bible for good because he made the mistake of starting at the wrong place and became discouraged by a succession of dull or difficult passages. There are gates through which you can enter the Bible most easily, sections which swing wide their doors with the least effort on your part. Then, once you are inside the book and familiar with its thoroughfares, you will be ready to find your way alone. There will be no more danger of your being lost. Let's try to find the best gates to the Bible.

The first thing to remember is that it is not necessary to start at the beginning and travel straight through. The Bible is a library of books, not a single book. You don't read a library by beginning at the first page of the book at the start of the top shelf. You browse around among the different titles until you see something that interests you. Or you ask the librarian for advice.

In deciding where to begin, it is well to remember how we happen to have the Bible. We have it as a world book because the first followers of Jesus, who were mostly Jews, preserved it and delivered it to us. To them the Old Testament told of the preparation for Christ's coming, and the

New Testament recorded the story of his arrival and the new beginnings in the life of the world which his life and teachings inaugurated.

If Jesus had not come it is likely that the magnificent literature of the Old Testament might never have been widely known outside the Jewish fellowship.

It seems logical then to begin your Bible reading with the New Testament, which was responsible for the wide dissemination of the whole book. The first four books of the New Testament preserve for us almost all we have in the Bible of the life of Christ, and they make a perfect beginning to the whole book. However, they should *not* be read in the order we have them in the Bible—Matthew, Mark, Luke and John.

One good reason why is illustrated by this story. One day a religious worker at the Great Lakes Naval Training Station saw a fine-looking lad, a new recruit, come to his post. The young man spied a stock of New Testaments for distribution and asked what they were. When he was told that the New Testament was a part of the Bible, he said he had heard of the Bible but had never seen a copy. The worker told him he would be glad to present him with a Testament if he would promise to read it. The sailor promptly accepted the offer and trudged off with his little book. At about the same hour the next day, however, the sailor was back with his Testament, saying he guessed he wouldn't read it after all. When asked why, he replied, "Well, I started in at the beginning, but I had to quit." He paused for a moment, then blurted out, "It reads just like a telephone book to me!"

It was clear what had happened. The sailor had begun to read the Testament as he would any other book—on page one. Almost the whole of the first page of the first gospel was a list of strange-looking names, seventeen verses of genealogy listing Jesus' family tree. He could not have started at a more discouraging place.

There are even better reasons for not beginning with Matthew than that it opens with a genealogy. Matthew was evidently not the first of the gospels to be written. Almost all scholars now believe that the earliest gospel was Mark. Therefore Mark is a logical beginning to the New Testament.

Another reason for beginning with Mark rather than Matthew is that Mark's is the shortest of the gospels and the simplest. The minute you start it you feel the zest and enthusiasm of the writer. He writes like a reporter covering an exciting World Series, with his side winning. He called what he was writing not a biographical sketch but "good news"—that's what the word "gospel" means. Every chapter vibrates with a sense of challenge and triumph as if Mark were saying, "Here is the story of a man who turned the whole world upside-down! Read about him; you'll never be the same!"

The gospel of Mark can be read in about an hour. It provides the best introduction to the earthly life of the greatest man who ever lived. Try reading it at one sitting, with no interruptions to stop the flow of the narrative. You will never forget the experience.

We have no reason to believe that Mark was a literary expert. But this plain man had something so momentous to say, something which burst out of him so explosively and spontaneously, that the cleverest literary craftsmen of all time have never produced anything to equal it.

After you have read Mark, it is time to read Matthew. Having become acquainted with Jesus, the genealogy with which Matthew opens may now interest you. Matthew must have had Mark's gospel before him when he wrote, for of Mark's 661 verses, Matthew uses 600. However, Matthew also looked around and found other sources on the life of Jesus to draw upon when writing. He gives us pages and pages of what Jesus said.

It is wonderful to read Matthew after Mark, for Mark leaves you asking, "What else did Jesus say on such and such an occasion?" In many cases Matthew tells you. Chapters 5, 6 and 7 in Matthew comprise the greatest sermon ever preached. We call it the Sermon on the Mount. It is the most concentrated statement of spiritual wisdom ever recorded. Here are a few excerpts:

> Therefore all things whatsoever ye would that men should do to you, do ye even so to them.

> Give not that which is holy unto the dogs, neither cast ye your pearls before swine, lest they trample them under their feet, and turn again and rend you.

> Enter ye in at the strait gate; for wide is the gate, and broad is the way, that leadeth to destruction, and many there be which go in thereat: because strait is the gate, and narrow is the way, which leadeth unto life, and few there be that find it.

> Judge not, that ye be not judged. For with what judgment ye judge, ye shall be judged; and with what measure ye mete, it shall be measured to you again.

> Ye have heard that it hath been said, "An eye for an eye, and a tooth for a tooth." But I say unto you, "That ye resist not evil: but whosoever shall smite thee on thy right cheek, turn to him the other also."

> Ye have heard that it hath been said, "Thou shalt love thy neighbour, and hate thine enemy." But I say unto you, "Love your enemies, bless them that curse you, do good to them that hate you, and pray for them which despitefully use you, and persecute you; that ye may be the children of your Father which is in heaven: for he maketh his sun to rise on the

evil and on the good, and sendeth rain on the just and on the unjust."

The Sermon on the Mount can be read and reread countless times. The more of it you know by heart, the more helpful it will be.

Matthew, however, was not the only one who found his inspiration to write of Jesus' life when he had read Mark's gospel. Apparently many others did besides, because when we turn to the next gospel, we find Luke, a Greek physician, beginning his gospel (which is really a long letter to his friend Theophilus) in this way:

> Inasmuch as many have undertaken to compile a narrative of the things which have been accomplished among us . . . it seemed good to me also . . . to write an orderly account for you . . . that you may know the truth concerning the things of which you have been informed.

And then Luke, also following Mark's outline much as Matthew did, starts in with the matchless stories about Jesus' birth. Luke is a literary artist. His nativity stories, and the tale of Jesus' visit as a boy to the Temple, are unforgettable. Of all the gospel writers, he alone gives us the parables of the Good Samaritan, the Lost Sheep, the Prodigal Son and Dives and Lazarus. It is Luke who so often shows us Jesus at prayer. From Luke the world gained a new respect for women. His is a gospel of good tidings, joy and the new power of the Holy Spirit.

Luke is the only non-Jewish author we know of in the Bible. Naturally, then, he looks on Jesus not only as the Messiah of the Jews but as the founder of Christianity. He is also the author of the book of The Acts which immediately follows the gospels.

It is a good idea to read the first three gospels in this order: Mark, Matthew, Luke, and then to skip to The Acts. It is really the sequel to Luke's gospel. The Acts is the most exciting piece of history ever written, and the only record we have of the time when the world was turning its big corner from ancient paganism toward the new ethical and moral concept in human relations which to this day we are still trying to perfect. Furthermore, The Acts introduces you to the foremost New Testament character next to Jesus himself—Paul the Apostle.

Paul dominates all but the few opening chapters of The Acts and is reflected also in the many letters he wrote, which comprise almost one fourth of the New Testament. We first meet him at the stoning of Stephen, the first Christian martyr, where we find him a bitter and determined enemy of Christ, with hatred in his heart.

When you read of his conversion a few weeks later—a story that is repeated twice later in The Acts—it is well to let your thoughts dwell on the true significance of the event. Here is a university graduate, a man of culture, personality and power, dramatically appointed by the risen Christ to interpret the gospel to the living generation. Here is a brilliant leader completely transformed, ready to reveal through his life and letters what Christ can do for the most wayward soul. Here is a man who took the new way of love and justice and mercy into the busy centers of the dying Roman Empire, and started men's thoughts flowing into those fresh channels that have led to our Christian civilization.

If Moses was the great man of the Old Testament because he gave God's basic moral law to his people, Paul is the great man of the New Testament because he interprets Christ's higher law of love for us. Here is what he says:

Let all bitterness, and wrath, and anger, and clamour, and evil speaking, be put away from you, with all malice: and

be ye kind one to another, tenderhearted, forgiving one another, even as God for Christ's sake hath forgiven you.

Be not deceived; God is not mocked; for whatsoever a man
soweth, that shall he also reap. For he that soweth to his
flesh shall of the flesh reap corruption; but he that soweth
to the spirit shall of the spirit reap life everlasting.

If I speak in the tongues of men and of angels, but have not
love, I am a noisy gong or a clanging cymbal. And if I have
prophetic powers, and understand all mysteries and all
knowledge, and if I have all faith, so as to remove mountains, but have not love, I am nothing. If I give away all I
have, and if I deliver my body to be burned, but have not
love, I gain nothing.

The gospel of John should be read after The Acts. To
many people John is the most priceless of all the books ever
written. It probably appeared many years after the other
gospels and The Acts. It reflects the power Jesus exerted
upon his own generation as well as what many feel is the
heart of Jesus' message to humanity. As John develops his
theme all else seems to fade into the background save Jesus
himself. As the reader, you seem to be alone with Christ, and
he seems to be speaking not to his disciples but to you, as in
those precious words of the fourteenth chapter, beginning:

Let not your hearts be troubled; believe in God, believe also
in me. In my Father's house are many rooms; if it were not
so, would I have told you that I go to prepare a place for
you? And when I go and prepare a place for you, I will come
again and will take you to myself, that where I am you may
be also. And you know the way where I am going.
    Thomas said to him, "Lord, we do not know where you
are going; how can we know the way?"
    Jesus said to him, "I am the way, and the truth, and the
life; no one comes to the Father, but by me."

You can read the gospel of John in less than two hours, but so rich are the words in comfort and guidance and revelation that they continue to satisfy you through the rereadings of a lifetime.

If you begin your Bible reading with the five books mentioned in this order: Mark, Matthew, Luke, The Acts, John, you will have made the best of all possible beginnings. These are the five books against which all the others must be evaluated. As you continue your reading from there, remember always that the Bible is a library, perfect for browsing around. When you have finished reading the present book, you will have definite ideas as to what other books of the Bible appeal to you most. Trust those ideas, and read where your interest leads you.

A good beginning is to set aside a little time for reading the Bible every day. Try to build the habit by thinking of it as a daily appointment with God. Try to feel as if you were due to meet someone through your reading, someone you must not keep waiting.

This daily reading, as we mentioned earlier, has some pitfalls and you must be careful to avoid them. It is possible for your daily reading to become an arduous task, a strait jacket, which will rob you of all real pleasure and profit. To avoid this, try not to make hard work of reading the Bible.

Do not come to it as a task. Come to it with the spirit of Mary, the sister of Martha and Lazarus, who sat at Jesus' feet and drank in his words. Read as if you were listening to the deep melodies of a great organ, and after a bit you will find your own heart singing a nobler tune. Relax as you read. Try to tune in on the true message of the Bible which runs through its thousands of words.

Refrain from setting yourself a certain number of chapters to read at each setting. Read as the spirit moves you, and as far as it moves you. When you have heard and felt enough for one day, put down the Bible and go about your daily work. In reading the Bible you are not cramming for an examination, but living with a friend. True friendship can never be forced, it must spring spontaneously from your heart.

No matter how full your life is now, you can find time every day for reading the Bible. Some of the busiest people in the world do this, and so can you. They have put Bible reading in the class with eating and sleeping—where it belongs.

Charles Dickens, in a letter to his youngest son, who was leaving home to join his brother in Australia, wrote, "I put a New Testament among your books for the very same reasons and with the very same hopes that made me write an easy account of it for you when you were a little child—because it is the best book that ever was or will be known in the world, and because it teaches you the best lessons by which any human creature who tries to be truthful and faithful to duty can possibly be guided."

Many people find that the best time for daily Bible reading is the first thing in the morning, others the last thing at night. We are all more likely to have privacy at those times.

Some people find a strange kind of privacy in the midst of a swarm of strangers, as when they are traveling to and from work. If you don't want to carry a whole Bible to your job every day, you can carry a little book containing the Psalms or Proverbs or one of the Prophets or the gospels. The whole Bible is available in this form in twenty-two little volumes from the American Bible Society.

Many of the texts with which you begin the day will remain fixed in your memory, and will be a source of strength and guidance just when you need them most.

A business man recently said, "Sometimes in the morning I am appalled by all the duties and appointments that await me in the next ten hours. Then I repeat to myself these texts of the Bible: *In quietness and in confidence shall be your strength,* and *Thou wilt keep him in perfect peace, whose mind is stayed on thee.* It is astonishing," he said, "how quickly the load is lifted when I become aware of God's presence. The strain and tension vanish and there wells up within me a feeling of serenity and peace."

Here are three selections from the Bible which many find to be a source of strength when they are worried or fearful or facing a crisis:

> God is our refuge and strength,
> A very present help in trouble.
> Therefore will not we fear, though the earth be removed,
> And though the mountains be carried into the midst of the sea.

> But where shall wisdom be found?
> And where is the place of understanding?
> Man does not know the way to it,
> And it is not found in the land of the living . . .
> God understands the way to it,
> And he knows its place.
> For he looks to the ends of the earth,
> And sees everything under the heavens.

> I will lift up mine eyes unto the hills,
> From whence cometh my help.
> My help cometh from the Lord,
> Which made heaven and earth.

Too many people turn to their Bibles only in times of trouble. But in Bible reading, as in medicine, an ounce of prevention is worth a pound of cure. If you take your Bible as a regular daily food, you will find it nourishing and sustaining. It becomes part of you. It is the source of your moral strength. As Helen Keller said, "Unless we form the habit of going to the Bible in bright moments as well as in trouble, we cannot fully respond to its consolations, because we lack equilibrium between light and darkness."

Once your Bible has become part of you, through daily reading, you will find yourself changing as a person. You will notice it is easier to approach other people, to hold your tongue and your temper, to find serenity and composure, to understand the other fellow better and make him understand you. The old fears that used to embarrass you in the presence of the boss or of strangers or critics, will no longer overpower you. You will find a new freedom. As the Bible says, "If you continue in my word . . . you will know the truth and the truth will make you free."

Read expectantly, with an open mind. As you read, ask yourself, "What is God's message for me today?" Dispel from your mind every thought of the application of this message to other people. This is God's message for you alone. The more you are willing to listen, the more he will say.

Ask yourself, "What does this passage teach me to believe? —to become?—to do?" You may be reading a Psalm. Make the psalmist's words your own as when he says,

> Wash me thoroughly from my iniquity,
> And cleanse me from my sin!
> For I know my transgressions,
> And my sin is ever before me.

Some of the trouble with people, so the psychiatrists tell us, is that they are nursing a sense of guilt. Like a festering sore, it needs to be lanced and relieved. Bible reading can become a confessional that helps you do this, if you read expectantly and with a desire for guidance.

Read with imagination and unhurriedly. There is no reason to feel that you must cover a certain amount of territory in your Bible every day. You may benefit more from reading two verses because you honestly want to, than from making yourself read a whole chapter. The important thing is to understand and apply what you read. Often the meaning in a short passage will have a greater effect if you let it develop in your mind.

Robert Louis Stevenson wrote about the New Testament, "I believe it would startle and move anyone if they could make a certain effort of imagination and read it freshly like a book, not droningly or dully like a portion of the Bible."

People often complain that the Bible is too long. Actually, one of the real difficulties in reading it is that it is so short. It condenses whole lifetimes into a few powerful paragraphs. It distills the greatest thoughts into a line or two. It is then up to you to expand it. A parable which Jesus may have told in a score of words can easily be enlarged into a whole book or feature film—and many have been. The brief story of Joseph, told in fourteen chapters of the Bible, has been expanded into a four-volume novel by the late Thomas Mann.

Take the First Psalm. It has thirteen lines. It can be read aloud in thirty seconds. Here it is:

> Blessed is the man
> Who walks not in the counsel of the wicked,
> Nor stands in the way of sinners,
> Nor sits in the seat of scoffers;
> But his delight is in the law of the Lord,
> And on his law he meditates day and night.
> He is like a tree
> Planted by streams of water,

That yields its fruit in its season,
And its leaf does not wither.
In all that he does, he prospers.
The wicked are not so,
But are like chaff which the wind drives away.
Therefore the wicked will not stand in the judgment,
Nor sinners in the congregation of the righteous;
For the Lord knows the way of the righteous,
But the way of the wicked will perish.

Now stop to think about the Psalm. It draws the picture
of two men. One has learned that there are some things
which are out of bounds in life. He must avoid taking advice
from men who have no place for God in their lives. He must
not listen to men who are cynical. He has learned that the
best life has in it certain great refusals.

The other man is called the wicked man who *does* walk
in the counsel of the wicked and stand in the way of sinners
and sit in the seat of scoffers.

The psalmist likens the wise man to a tree that is planted
by a river. He describes the tree. It has vitality, fertility,
steadfastness, fruitfulness, charm and unending prosperity.
By contrast, he describes the wicked man as a stalk of worth-
less chaff that is dead, dry, helpless, useless, with no perma-
nence and no fruit.

As you continue to let your imagination play on these
verses, you ask what makes the difference between these two
men. And the answers come up out of the Psalm like the sun
in the morning. It says the good man's "delight is in the law
of the Lord and in his law he meditates day and night." That
brings you right out where you yourself are, enjoying reading
"the law of the Lord" and, in fact, meditating on it.

*Mark passages that are not clear and come back to them
later.* Not all the Bible is so simple and beautiful as the First

Psalm or some of the stories Jesus told. Some parts will not be clear to you on first reading them. Mark them, perhaps with a question mark, and come back to them later. Something else you have read in the meantime and whose meaning is clear may throw light on the baffling passages. There are, of course, some passages that you may never come to understand. Even professional Bible students are sometimes not clear about them. This is not strange in view of the fact that the Bible was written long ago by people whose lives were cast in an entirely different mold. The amazing thing is that there is so little in the Bible that is not perfectly clear.

Mark Twain once listened to a friend complain that there was so much in the Bible he could not understand. "Oh," replied Mark Twain, "it's the parts of the Bible that I *can* understand that worry me."

When you read your Bible, keep your pencil in hand. There is nothing so sacred about your copy of the Bible that it should not be marked with your records. Put down the thoughts that come to you as you read. Your marginal notes can be a log of discovery on your voyage.

Bible reading helps your soul to grow. The notes you make in the margin of your Bible may become like the marks you made on the door-post when you were a growing child. When you come back to read the same passage a year later, you may find that you have grown perceptibly in spiritual appreciation and insight. By such practices as this, your Bible will become more valuable as the years go by. It will become a personal record of your search for the truth.

Read and reread passages that particularly appeal to you. Perhaps they have a haunting beauty of phrase. Or they sum up some truth you have been seeking but which has always eluded you. You may even want to memorize them.

The more of the Bible you have made your own, the greater force it can become in your life. William Gladstone, the famous British leader, once said, "On most occasions of very sharp pressure or trial, some word of scripture has come to me as if borne on angels' wings."

Here are a few verses well worth remembering:

Let the words of my mouth and the meditation of my heart
Be acceptable in thy sight,
O Lord, my rock and my redeemer.

Trust in the Lord with all thine heart; and lean not unto thine own understanding. In all thy ways acknowledge him, and he shall direct thy paths.

Watch and pray, that ye enter not into temptation; the spirit indeed is willing, but the flesh is weak.

I am the way, the truth, and the life: no man cometh unto the Father, but by me.

In the world you have tribulation; but be of good cheer, I have overcome the world.

Whatsoever things are true, whatsoever things are honest, whatsoever things are just, whatsoever things are pure, whatsoever things are lovely, whatsoever things are of good report; if there be any virtue, and if there be any praise, think on these things . . . and the God of peace shall be with you.

I can do all things through Christ which strengtheneth me.

Besides verses like these, scattered throughout the text like bright stars in the sky, you will probably want to memorize the Twenty-third Psalm. This is the best-known poem ever written, and considered by many to be the most beautiful:

The Lord is my shepherd; I shall not want.
He maketh me to lie down in green pastures; he leadeth me
    beside the still waters.

He restoreth my soul; he leadeth me in the paths of righteousness for his name's sake.

Yea, though I walk through the valley of the shadow of
death, I will fear no evil; for thou art with me; thy rod
and thy staff they comfort me.

Thou preparest a table before me in the presence of mine
enemies: thou anointest my head with oil; my cup run-
neth over.

Surely goodness and mercy shall follow me all the days of
my life: and I will dwell in the house of the Lord for ever.

The Beatitudes, which open Christ's Sermon on the
Mount, are words you have heard since childhood. But perhaps they have not been added permanently to the store-
house of your mind. Now is the time to do it. There are no
finer riches for the mind. The Beatitudes comprise the first
twelve verses of the fifth chapter of the gospel of Matthew.

Paul's first letter to the Corinthians gives what is probably
the most accurate description of true love that has ever been
set down. We would all do well to ponder it often:

Love is very patient, very kind. Love knows no jealousy;
love makes no parade, gives itself no airs, is never rude, never
selfish, never irritated, never resentful; love is never glad
when others go wrong, love is gladdened by goodness, always
slow to expose, always eager to believe the best, always hope-
ful, always patient.

When earnest Christians gather together, their leader often
asks each one to repeat his favorite verse of scripture. The
response is invariably a collection of the great, reassuring
promises of the Bible. Here are a few of these precious promises:

The Lord is near to all who call upon him, to all who call
upon him in truth.

He fulfils the desire of all who fear him, he also hears their
cry and saves them.

No temptation has overtaken you that is not common to man. God is faithful, and he will not let you be tempted beyond your strength, but with the temptation will also provide the way of escape, that you may be able to endure it.

The Lord is near to the brokenhearted, and saves the crushed in spirit.

The angel of the Lord encamps around those who fear him, and delivers them.

But seek first his kingdom and his righteousness, and all these things shall be yours as well.

But they who wait for the Lord shall renew their strength,
They shall mount up with wings like eagles,
They shall run and not be weary,
They shall walk and not faint.

Peace I leave with you; my peace I give to you; not as the world gives do I give to you. Let not your hearts be troubled, neither let them be afraid.

If we confess our sins, he is faithful and just, and will forgive our sins and cleanse us from all unrighteousness.

But the fruit of the Spirit is love, joy, peace, patience, kindness, goodness, faithfulness, gentleness, self-control; against such there is no law.

Come to me, all who labor and are heavy-laden, and I will give you rest. Take my yoke upon you, and learn from me; for I am gentle and lowly in heart, and you will find rest for your souls. For my yoke is easy, and my burden is light.

As a father pities his children, so the Lord pities those who fear him.

Be strong and of good courage, do not fear or be in dread of them; for it is the Lord your God who goes with you; he will not fail you or forsake you.

Fear not, for I am with you,
Be not dismayed, for I am your God;

I will strengthen you, I will help you,
I will uphold you with my victorious right hand.

But he said to me, "My grace is sufficient for you, for my power is made perfect in weakness." I will all the more gladly boast of my weaknesses, that the power of Christ may rest upon me.

The true light that enlightens every man was coming into the world.

Thou dost keep him in perfect peace, whose mind is stayed on thee, because he trusts in thee.

For many Christians, there is no verse in the Bible that surpasses the sixteenth verse of the third chapter of John's gospel. It might be called the heart of the Bible:

For God so loved the world, that he gave his only Son, that whoever believes in him should not perish but have eternal life.

The more of the Bible you know by heart, the more you will be able to carry around with you always. Such passages can be a shield, a suit of armor, helping you in times of trouble or temptation, giving you a lift, opening the door to new achievements. They can raise your spirits in times of special need when no Bible is handy.

William Allen White, famous editor of the *Emporia Gazette,* wrote, "Every time I pick up the Bible, and I pick it up frequently in the course of a busy life, I find some new quotation which I can use until I pick it up again."

Read your Bible for pure enjoyment. "Reading the Bible for Fun," was the title of an article that appeared in a church paper a few years ago. It shocked some readers. To them the Bible was too holy to be thought of as a source of mere pleasure. But this is an approach to the Bible that is very much needed. Almost every guide to Bible reading omits the idea of reading it for sheer pleasure. A sort of shadow rests upon Bible reading because we are told that it is our pious duty to do it, that we will pile up merits if we do a few verses a day, whether we want to or not.

But much of it can be a great joy: the poetry of the Psalms, for instance, or the book of Proverbs in one of the modern English translations like Moffatt or Smith-Goodspeed. These translations give the Proverbs the sort of pithy, practical good sense that makes newspaper columnists such good reading. A single phrase from its salty pages will often get you off to a good day's start:

A merry heart doeth good like a medicine.

Wisdom is the principal thing; therefore get wisdom. She is more precious than rubies. The fear of the Lord is the beginning of wisdom.

A good name is rather to be chosen than great riches.

He that is soon angry dealeth foolishly. He that is slow to wrath is of great understanding. A soft answer turneth away wrath.

One man gives freely, yet grows all the richer; another withholds what he should give, and only suffers want.

The way of a fool is right in his own eyes but a wise man listens to advice.

Among the apocryphal books of the Bible (see page 164 for a discussion of these) is a book of wise observations much like Proverbs. It was written later, however, probably in the Roman era. It is called Ecclesiasticus, or the Wisdom of Sirach. As Dr. Edgar J. Goodspeed says, the author of this book "must have been a leading citizen of the old city [Jerusalem]; he went out to large dinners, he traveled widely, he observed

shrewdly and yet kindly. He loved nature and had a sense
of beauty; at the same time he saw deeply into the meaning
of work and saw that the farmer and the craftsman supported
the fabric of the world, and their prayer was in the practice
of their trade. He felt the beauty of the Temple services as
no one had ever done before. We would call him a church-
goer. At the same time he was religiously devoted to the
pursuit of wisdom, and over many years recorded his keen
observations in philosophic verse."

Many passages in this fascinating book sound like the writings of a current columnist, especially in Dr. Goodspeed's
modern translation. In one place the writer gives advice to
masters of ceremonies at large dinners and to after-dinner
speakers in general. He says:

> Speak concisely; say much in few words;
> Act like a man who knows more than he says.
>
> Prepare what you have to say, and then you will
> be listened to.

This wise counselor also had ideas about good dinner manners:

> Do not rebuke your neighbor at a banquet,
> And do not despise him in his mirth;
> Do not say a reproachful word to him,
> And do not press him to repay you.
> Be ashamed to lean on your elbow at table.

For sheer enjoyment the two small Bible books which bear
the names of women—Ruth and Esther—are incomparable.
Both books were written for a definite purpose; Ruth, as a
protest against the narrow nationalist doctrine which forbade
a Jew to marry a wife of non-Jewish family, and Esther, to
encourage the observance of the joyous festival of Purim,
when Jews gave dinners for their friends and made gifts to

one another. However, the purpose behind the writing of the two books is somewhat overshadowed by the great narrative skill of the authors. These are enthralling, moving short stories, a delight from beginning to end.

Another book that is a joy to read is the book of Jonah. This book is misunderstood by many readers because so much emphasis has been placed on the big fish that swallows the hero. Actually the real purpose of the book is a broadminded one: to emphasize the fact that God cares for other people and nations besides the Jews.

Have you ever thought of adapting your Bible reading to the seasons of the year? What better time to read the book that gave us Christmas—than at Christmastime? It offers a perfect opportunity to introduce the charm of the Bible into your family circle. You can make it a part of your Christmas celebration by listening with your family to the opening chapters of Matthew and Luke. Perhaps you can take turns reading it, children included. The chances are that when your family members find they enjoy reading the Bible together, they will clamor for more. There is no surer way of giving your children a lifelong love for the Bible than to show them how it can be read and enjoyed by all of you together. Children almost always enjoy things that their family does together, and Bible reading is no exception.

Good Friday and Easter are also perfect times for introducing the Bible into your family circle. And on Thanksgiving you might read some of the Psalms of thanksgiving—numbers 40, 46, 48, 67, 107 and 124.

The letter of Paul to the Galatians lends itself to reading on Independence Day. This letter has been called the charter of religious freedom, which is of course the basic freedom of them all.

Chapter 7

The Best Edition and Translation
for You

IT IS essential to supply yourself with a good, readable copy of the Bible. This is not as easy as it sounds. There are more editions of the English Bible available in America today than of any other book at any time in any country on earth. Maybe you will want to ask your pastor's advice on the matter. Or you may want to go to your local bookstore and browse around the shelves. Your bookseller can also give you the names and addresses of the standard publishers of the Bible, and you can write them for a more complete and detailed listing of the various editions. You are going to live with your Bible for a long time, so be sure to buy the one that suits you best. A big "must" is that your Bible be not too big for comfortable handling and that the type be clear and bold.

One of the first things to strike you about most of the Bibles published today is the fact that the pages are printed in double columns of type, rather than in single columns like this book and most other books. The reason lies in the Bible's length. If it were printed like most other books, it would require about five ordinary "hand-sized" volumes. Therefore, it is necessary to print more words to a page. The type in narrow columns can be smaller and closer together, because your eye can easily jump back across a short line without losing the place. This is why most Bibles are printed in two narrow columns rather than one wide one. The Bible is not the only book printed in this narrow-column way: our popular magazines and all our newspapers use narrow columns to save space too.

Another striking fact about the Bible is that many editions are peppered with big and little numbers. These are the chapters and verses of the Bible; for example, the citation Genesis VI:1 refers to Chapter 6, Verse 1, of the book of Genesis.

The early printed editions (like the famous Gutenberg Bible of 1456, first to be issued) were not divided into a minute system of chapters and verses. The first printed scripture volume so divided was issued in France in 1527. Robert Stephens, member of a famous family of scholars and printers, followed the practice in his edition of the New Testament in 1551. Stephens' system was adopted by the English scholars who translated the Bible in Geneva, bringing out the New Testament in 1557 and the entire Bible in 1560. This Geneva Bible, as it was called, became immensely popular in England, and from it stemmed the tradition of division into chapters and verses.

Some of the Bible editions you find in the bookstores and libraries do not bear these numbers. Their editors, in reprinting the Bible, felt that the thousands of numbers impeded the free flow of your reading, and were better omitted. However, these chapter-and-verse divisions have an advantage, too. They enable you to find certain passages quickly. For instance, at the back of this book, you will find handy reference-lists of some of the best-loved songs, prayers, stories and benedictions of the Bible. Of course you must locate them in the long text by chapter and verse, and if your edition omits all or part of these divisions you may have a hard time finding them.

At any rate, when you decide on what special edition of the Bible to buy for your own adventuring in the text, take this matter of chapter-and-verse divisions into account.

Another reason why some editions of the Bible have a weird and rather discouraging appearance lies in the fact that they are so-called "self-pronouncing editions." That means that proper nouns—names of places and persons—are marked to show syllable division, where the stress falls, and sometimes how vowels are to be pronounced. For example the word "Josiah" might be shown as "Jō-sī'-ah" whenever it appears in the text. Since many of the proper nouns in the Bible are so unfamiliar in spelling and appearance, we can get no idea of their pronunciation by merely looking at them. Therefore some early Bible editors clarified the pronunciations right in the text, thus saving the conscientious reader the trouble of consulting a Bible dictionary or index. There are pros and cons to this editorial device in Bible publishing. You will want to decide for yourself whether pronunciation marks interrupt your reading flow and give the text a dictionary flavor, or whether the correct pronunciation in the book helps you.

Another way in which publishers add to the Bible text itself: the references and cross-references. You will find that some Bibles carry footnotes or marginal notes alongside or below certain passages. Such notes refer you to another part of the Bible where the text has a bearing on the passage you are reading. For instance, in a King James reference edition of the Bible published by the Oxford University Press, we find the small italic reference letter "o" just before the expression "he leadeth me in the paths of righteousness" in the Twenty-third Psalm. In the references found in a narrow center column beside this verse we find near the little "o," this reference: Psalms 5:8; 31:3 and Proverbs 8:20. When we look up these verses we find that they all refer to the idea of God's leading people in the paths of righteousness.

Cross-references are mainly of interest to the Bible scholar or the very serious student. It is doubtful that many will be helpful for your reading purposes—at least, in the beginning. You will probably want to make sure your edition either carries no references or places them so they do not interfere with your reading.

In most editions of the King James Version will be found occasional words or phrases printed in italics. This may be confusing to the beginner until he learns the reason for them. They are not used for emphasis, as in other books. They are used where the translators were unable to find English words precisely equivalent to some of the words in the Hebrew, Aramaic and Greek which they were translating. Also, wherever they were compelled to insert extra words to make the translation intelligible to English readers they put these additional words in italics to indicate the insertions. They were meticulous translators.

The absence of quotation marks in most editions of the King James Versions may also disturb the beginner. The explanation of this is that quotation marks, which originated in France during the late sixteenth century, had not been generally adopted by English printers when the King James Version was first issued in 1611. So strong has tradition been that, to this day, virtually all regular editions of the King James Version use no quotation marks.

So much for additions to and variations of the text itself.

Bibles are published today with all kinds of helpful material both before and after the text.

For instance, some come with a concordance between the

covers. A concordance is an index showing the places in the Bible where the principal words are found, a device which enables you to locate a particular passage. For example, if you want to know the place in the books of The Acts where, because the Apostle Paul preached so long one night in a second floor hall, one of his hearers fell asleep and fell out of the window, you look in the concordance for the word "window." There you will find perhaps a dozen places where the word occurs in the Bible. Among them you will find these words, "there sat in a *window* a certain young man. Acts 20:9." You have located your story.

Many concordances are separate volumes which go so far as to list every word in the Bible, even the word "and," telling you all places where each occurs.

Another reading-help sometimes bound into the Bible, and at other times published separately, is a Bible dictionary. This gives you a brief description of all the names and places and proper nouns that you will come across, plus other useful information. One of the latest to appear is called *Harper's Bible Dictionary*, a fascinating volume, well illustrated.

There are Bibles with maps of Bible lands, and with introductions and outlines for the books, lists of the miracles, the parables, the divine promises, brief sketches of the lives of principal characters, and a great variety of other helps. Check different editions for these reading-aids. They can substantially improve the ease of your reading.

There are also many editions of the Bible with pictures. The American Bible Society recently published an edition of the New Testament under the title, *The Good News,* which is profusely illustrated with over five hundred pictures, besides maps and charts. The captions of the pictures shed further light on the accompanying text. Many of the photographs were taken especially for this edition.

The whole Bible is of course available in Braille and in

other embossed systems for the blind. For those who cannot read with their fingers, it may be heard on a set of Talking Book records.

For those who wish to carry their Bible with them, there are not only pocket-size entire Bibles, which necessarily means that the type is very small, but little separate volumes bound in stout canvas covers that can be carried easily. The New Testament alone is available in many small, attractive pocket sizes.

The Bible is a cosmopolitan book. It can be bought not only in English but in almost any other language you may want. Each year copies of the scriptures are sold in the United States in more than seventy-five languages. In the English language it is available in those translations that are most commonly used by Protestants, Catholics and Jews.

In the next section of this book, in the chapter titled, "How the Bible Came to Us in English," we sketch the origin of the important English translations in use today. Here, therefore, we will touch only briefly on the translations which are available to you and the special reading qualities of each. However, since no description can possibly capture their true flavor, here is a suggestion. Go to the library and do a little reading in each of the Bible translations we mention here. Compare the same passages in every book—not one of your favorite passages, because your ear will already be accustomed to a certain phrasing, but a new and untried passage. See which one suits you best. Most of the famous Bible passages you have been hearing all your life are taken from the King James, or Authorized, Version of 1611, but that does not make it essential that you cling to this version today. Perhaps a more modern translation, with less literary value but more clarity of phrase and wording, will mean more to you.

Do a little sleuthing on your own before investing money in one translation. Or, if you cannot make up your mind, and find value and beauty equally in two translations, you may want to buy both.

There are three so-called "standard texts" or translations among Protestant Bibles. They are called standard texts because they have been the work of officially appointed scholars, representing the various branches of Protestantism.

The King James Version, published in the year 1611, is the most popular among Protestants today, and it has enjoyed an unrivaled popularity for centuries. It has been termed "the noblest monument of English prose" and with good reason. It is certainly the greatest translation from a purely literary standpoint that has ever been made. It has simplicity, dignity and power. It is full of admirable rhythms, a ringing organ-tone of sound. At its mightiest moments its language rises effortlessly and unerringly to supreme heights. It is probably our greatest literary heritage.

Here are just a few memorable passages from the King James Version, words that seem to echo in the ear long after we have heard them:

> Consider the lilies of the field, how they grow; they toil not, neither do they spin: and yet I say unto you, That even Solomon in all his glory was not arrayed like one of these.

> I am distressed for thee, my brother Jonathan:
> Very pleasant hast thou been unto me:
> Thy love to me was wonderful,
> Passing the love of women.
> How are the mighty fallen,
> And the weapons of war perished!

> When I was a child, I spake as a child, I understood as a child, I thought as a child: but when I became a man, I put away childish things. For now we see through a glass, darkly;

but then face to face: now I know in part; but then shall I know even as also I am known. And now abideth faith, hope, charity, these three; but the greatest of these is charity.

However, the King James Version has certain defects for readers today, and these must be weighed in the balance. Today, through archaeological research and discoveries, we possess manuscripts that are much older and immensely more reliable than those on which the King James translators based their work. The newer Bible translations, of course, are based on these more recently uncovered texts. For example, the King James Version of the New Testament was based on a Greek text that had gone through fourteen centuries of copying by hand! By that time it had been marred by many mistakes, which of course the King James translation reflected.

Another defect of the King James Version is the state of linguistic scholarship at the time of its creation. In the last hundred years scholars have made many new discoveries about the ancient tongues in which the Bible was first set down. Today we have a much more accurate idea of word meanings and sentence structure in those languages than did the King James translators. This means that many of the King James renderings can be improved upon from the standpoint of accuracy.

However, the major reason for considering more modern translations than the King James for yourself is the change since 1611 in English usage. Some of the archaic forms of expression in the King James Bible are not objectionable: for instance, its use of thou, thee, thy, thine and the verb endings -est and -edst, -eth and -th, and expressions such as "it came to pass that," "whosoever," etc., all of which lend a very special flavor and tone that many readers rightly treasure. The trouble arises rather from the fact that a large number of the English words used by the translators have changed their meaning over the years. They no longer convey the thoughts the translators originally charged them with. For example, the King James Version uses the word "let" to mean "hinder"; "prevent" to mean "precede"; "allow" to mean "approve"; "communicate" for "share"; "wealth" for "well-being"; "allege" for "prove"; "demand" for "ask"; "take no thought" for "be not anxious"; and many more. The Greek word for "immediately" is variously translated "anon," "by and by" and "presently." There are more than three hundred such English words which are used in the King James Version in a sense quite different from that which they now carry. This state of affairs sometimes makes for unnecessary obscurity.

The other "standard" English texts in common use by American Protestants are the American Revised Version, first published in 1901, a revision of the King James Version; and the Revised Standard Version which came out in 1952 and which, while virtually a new translation from the Hebrew and Greek, has preserved as far as possible the familiar beauty of the King James language. However, the archaic forms of pronouns and verbs have been dropped in favor of more modern usage except in address to the Deity. No modern English translation has ever enjoyed as great an initial popularity as the Revised Standard Version. Many leading denominations have adopted it officially and over four million copies were sold within four years of its first printing.

Whether the literary supremacy of the King James Version will outweigh its defects is a decision only you can make. The important thing is to approach all translations with an open mind, remembering that the one which carries the burden of the Bible message most directly to your heart is the right one. However, if you are helping a young person understand and enjoy the Bible, you might do better to start him out on a modern translation, like the Revised Standard Version, since young people seem to have the greatest difficulty with the King James Version.

Besides the three standard texts mentioned above, there are many other English translations made by independent scholars for Protestant readers. These depart far more freely from the King James tradition of language and style. While they without doubt clear up obscurities and archaisms in the text, they differ substantially from all "standard" versions. The two most popular are *The Holy Bible: A New Translation* by James Moffatt and *The Bible: An American Translation* by J. M. P. Smith, Edgar J. Goodspeed, and others. These two books are available in most bookstores and libraries. There are two other excellent New Testaments in modern English: one, *The New Testament in Modern Speech* by Richard Francis Weymouth, a British scholar, and the other, *The Centenary New Testament,* the only widely recognized English translation made by a woman, Helen Barrett Montgomery.

For the reader interested in comparing the King James text with the modern independent translations, there are two editions of the New Testament printed in parallel columns—the King James text in one column and a modern version in the other. The books in each case are called the Parallel New Testament. One uses the Moffatt text and the other the Goodspeed text.

A still more radical type of modern translation of the New Testament has recently come from the pen of a brilliant English vicar, J. B. Phillips. So far three volumes have appeared. One is called *Letters to Young Churches* and is a free translation of all twenty-one Epistles of the New Testament. The second, called *The Gospels, Translated into Modern English,* contains the first four books of the New Testament. The third called *The Young Church in Action* is a fascinating translation of The Acts. The only book not included in the three volumes is the book of Revelation.

The standard Catholic English Bible is the one commonly known as the Douai Bible. This translation was made from the Latin Vulgate at about the same time as the King James, and was thoroughly revised in 1749 by Bishop Richard Challoner of London. There have been several later revisions.

In 1941 a revised and modernized version of the Challoner New Testament was published, edited by Catholic scholars under the patronage of the Episcopal Committee of the Confraternity of Christian Doctrine; and more recently there has appeared the first of two volumes of the Old Testament in the same revision.

The English version of the Old Testament now most widely used by English-speaking Jews in this country is the one published in 1917 by the Jewish Publication Society of America. Some, however, still prefer to use the text prepared in 1853 by Isaac Leeser, the first complete English Old Testament for Jewish readers. The Jewish Bible (Old Testament) differs from the King James in that instead of thirty-nine books it lists only twenty-four. However, this is only a difference of arrangement, for no books have been omitted. Instead, Samuel I and II are reckoned as one book, Kings I and II and Chronicles I and II likewise; Ezra and Nehemiah are combined and the twelve minor prophets are included as one book.

At the back of this book you will find a partial listing of special editions of the Bible that are currently available in libraries and bookstores. This list will give you an idea of the various formats in which thoughtful and devoted publishers have clothed the text. If you do not already have a

Bible in your home, or if the Bible you own does not employ modern typography and design to encourage your reading, we suggest you consult this list before buying another Bible.

One last suggestion: why not establish a special Bible shelf in your home? There you can assemble all pertinent reading matter. As you go on with your Bible reading you will find yourself adding new books to this shelf as well as articles, leaflets and tracts. It is good to have them all in one place. And no doubt you will want to add a second, or even third, translation of the text to your Bible shelf, as you discover that each translation has its own merits and can unlock the meaning of different passages.

Here is a brief summary of the important points we have covered in this section. They add up to all the hints you need on how to approach the Bible for help and guidance. Try to incorporate at least some of them into your new excursion into the Bible.

1. Begin your Bible reading with the New Testament, preferably in this order: Mark, Matthew, Luke, The Acts, John and then the Epistles and Revelation. As you continue your reading from there, always remember that the Bible is a library, not a single book. You can browse around in it to find sections that especially appeal to you. Read only as far as your interest carries you. You can always come back later to passages you omit now, as your understanding of the Bible and consequent appreciation of it grow.

2. Try to set aside a little time for Bible reading every single day. But do not come to your daily reading as a task. If you find yourself doing so, examine your attitudes toward the Bible and your reasons for reading it—and try to reach a more free, more spontaneous approach.

3. Read expectantly and with an open mind. Ask yourself,

"What is God's message for me today?" Try to turn the Bible's word into an active plan for living and doing, to help you become a better person.

4. Read with imagination and unhurriedly. Fill out the Bible's brief stories and descriptions with your own thoughts. Picture the scene as you read, and think of the characters as living people.

5. Don't be afraid to mark your Bible with thoughts that occur to you as you read. This conserves the results of your reading, and makes permanent the impressions you have received.

6. Memorize helpful passages or copy key verses to carry with you for reference throughout the day. Read with the definite purpose of making the Bible a practical guide to life. Sometimes you will be startled by what God says to you in the morning. You will get messages that meet the deepest needs of your life, that will send you forth with head erect and a brave heart.

7. Read the Bible for the pure enjoyment you can get out of it.

8. Be sure to take down your Bible at the great festive seasons of Christmas and Easter and share the book's story of these events with your family.

9. Decide on the translation of the Bible that is best for you, remembering that different translations hold different benefits. Also, examine the various editions of the Bible, each offering different printing formats, aids, and arrangements of the text, to select the one through which the light of the Bible shines brightest for you.

10. Equip yourself with a few standard Bible helps. These should include at least a concordance and a Bible dictionary.

PART THREE

The Background of the Bible

Chapter 8

The Golden Thread

SINCE WE are separated from the people of the Bible by a gulf of time, tongue, custom and history, no one can expect to plunge into its pages and find every event self-explanatory. There are certain to be difficulties due to our lack of familiarity with the circumstances of those days.

That is not to say, of course, that the Bible does not transcend these barriers and speak to us in fresh accents. It does. But reading your Bible can be still more rewarding if you take the time to investigate the time and scene in which it is set.

That is the purpose of this section: not to present itself as the key to your Bible (only *you* can be that key), but simply as an added help. We will cover three large areas of background information:

1) The physical geography of the Bible lands
2) The secular history of the era covered by the Bible— about 1200 B.C. to A.D. 100
3) The authorship of the Bible

Of course, we cannot exhaust any of these subjects. Our hope is to introduce you to each generally, and prove that the more you know about them, the more rewarding your reading will be. Then you can add to your knowledge of these subjects by further reading as the years go by.

There is one big question we must try to answer before we

begin probing the background of the Bible. It is a question which, when answered, goes a long way toward explaining the whole Bible itself. Stated simply, it is, Why was the Bible written by the Hebrews? Why did the Hebrew people rather than the Egyptians or the Babylonians or the Greeks ponder the great questions of good and evil on earth and set down their answers?

The Hebrews had a quality of mind and spirit that was unique in the ancient world. They were not empire-builders like the Assyrians. They were not artists and artisans like the Egyptians. They did not devise alphabets or astronomical systems. Nor did they have Rome's passion for order and organization.

Instead they had another gift. They had the power to discern and believe in God. They were possessed by the overwhelming idea that God did exist and did watch over them. The men and women who walk across the pages of the Bible were filled with the thought of God. Their uniqueness lay in their abiding fellowship with God.

But there is another point here, one that has had a profound effect on our Western beliefs. For the men and women of the Bible, God not only existed: he demanded righteousness. The Hebrews believed (and if they tended to forget, they were reminded by their prophets) that God expects *righteous behavior* of men. The Hebrews were among the first to be concerned with a question very much with us today: How shall I behave? How shall I fulfill my obligations toward my family, my neighbors, my country and my world? The answers they gave in the Bible are considered by many to be the most valid yet found, the answers rooted in the idea of a just and merciful God.

The consideration of this problem led thoughtful Hebrews to another closely related one. Why, they asked, may a man

live righteously, but find misfortune raining down on him?
Why, in this world, do the innocent sometimes suffer?

We read the Bible's answer in the book of Job, in the
prophecies of Micah and in many of the Psalms: the ways
of God need not be justified to man; it is sufficient that a
man live righteously and put his trust in a providence he
cannot always comprehend. This is clearly and beautifully
stated by the prophet Habakkuk:

> Behold, he whose soul is not upright in him shall fail,
> But the righteous shall live by his faith.

Later, he writes of his trust in God:

> Though the fig tree do not blossom,
> Nor fruit be on the vines,
> The produce of the olive fail
> And the fields yield no food,
> The flock be cut off from the fold
> And there be no herd in the stalls,
> Yet I will rejoice in the Lord,
> I will joy in the God of my salvation.

The New Testament, in the light of Christ's death and
resurrection, gives us a further answer to this question. All
suffering, Christianity teaches, has in it the seeds of achievement and blessing. Take the apostle Paul, for example.
When Paul and his companion were thrown in jail at Philippi, they didn't bemoan their fate. *They sang hymns.*
Their faith had given them the victory over suffering. As
someone has written, "Our religion does not change the
world, our religion changes men." That, in eleven words,
sums up the power of Christianity and makes the Bible "the
positive answer to the world's despair."

So when we ask, Why were the Hebrews the people who
wrote the Bible? we can reply, Because they were gifted with

the desire, first, to know God and build a code of behavior based on that knowledge, and, second, to prove that God's mercy and justice are unfailingly available.

This central theme of man and his relationship to God explains why so many things are left out of the Bible. It says almost nothing about the vast empires that rose and fell during the centuries covered by its story. Its concern is principally an insignificant nation tucked away in a corner of the Mediterranean, a nation most of the time a vassal of one great empire or another.

It says almost nothing about science, in a period when many discoveries about medicine and astronomy were taking place. It says nothing about great contemporaries like Plato, Socrates, Aristotle, or eastern religious leaders like Confucius and Buddha. All of these thinkers must have been known to some of the later biblical writers.

Where Greece was interested in art and mathematics and philosophy and science, and Rome was interested in government and conquest, Israel's absorption was in religion.

And this is the link that binds the Bible so closely together that it is customarily thought of not as a library of books but as a single book. This central theme of God's relationship to man is expressed and dramatized in many different ways, but behind all the stories and poems and sermons, it is always there.

The Bible, therefore, reflects chiefly the thoughts of the Hebrews on God's redeeming love and a life of righteousness. But it also acquaints the reader with the country of its setting, the historical events of its day and the living habits of its people. It is these we shall investigate now.

Chapter 9

The Land of the Book

THE SETTING of the Bible is a long way from home. Its cities
and towns, valleys and rivers, cannot evoke a picture in your
mind, as do the words "Texas" or "Rocky Mountains." And
yet the places named in the Bible—the River Jordan, Samaria
(home of the Good Samaritan), the land of Canaan—are as
real and distinctive as any spot in America. It is important,
if your Bible reading is to have depth, that you be able to
carry in your mind the map of Bible lands and the location
of most of the place-names mentioned. The reasons for this
are twofold:

First, knowing the whereabouts of a certain plain or mountain or city makes the action come alive for you. For example, if you know where the Sinai Peninsula is, you are able to
form a clear picture of the wanderings of the Hebrew people
after they left Egypt. You know approximately how much
territory they covered, the nature of the terrain and how far
they would have to travel to reach the promised land to the
north.

Second, if you have a clear picture of the places mentioned,
it lights up the meaning of the passages in which they occur.
This is because place-names are often used as similies, for
literary effect:

> Behold, how good and how pleasant it is,
> For brethren to dwell together in unity!
> It is like . . . the dew of Hermon . . .
> That descended upon the mountains of Zion.

The waters of snow-capped Mount Hermon, to the north of the land of Israel, were welcome blessings to the parched land. They were, in fact, as welcome as the sight of men living together like brothers.

Another case where place-names are used to enrich the passage is in David's lament for Saul and Saul's son Jonathan. It contains these lines:

> The beauty of Israel is slain upon thy high places:
> How are the mighty fallen!
> Tell it not in Gath,
> Publish it not in the streets of Ashkelon;
> Lest the daughters of the Philistines rejoice.

The two cities, Gath and Ashkelon, belonged to the Philistines, enemies of the Hebrews.

Another example of the use of place-names for dramatic effect is in the passage describing the happy days of Solomon's rule: "And Judah and Israel dwelt safely, every man under his vine and under his fig tree, from Dan even to Beer-sheba, all the days of Solomon." This passage becomes clearer when we know that Dan was the northernmost city of the kingdom, and Beer-sheba the southernmost. The passage says that every man, bar none, was happy and safe. Our expression, "from Portland, Maine to Portland, Oregon," means the same thing.

The job of fixing in your mind the places mentioned in the Bible is easier than you might think, because most references in the Bible are accurate. The book is filled with names of places that either still exist or can be fixed quite clearly.

First, let us place the Bible land in its setting of the Old

World. The hard truth is that the little land was caught between the great empires of the Old World. It was a buffer
state between Egypt on the south, and Assyria, Babylonia,
Persia, Greece and Rome to the north.

What this means to a small nation is obvious from the fate
of Poland in modern times. Poland has been invaded, conquered, dismembered. Its cities have been ravaged and its
citizens exiled because it has been a highway between the
Eastern and the Western powers. The same was true of the
land of the Hebrews in Bible days. Later, we will sketch a
brief history of the nation. You will see how its vital and vul-
nerable position was a temptation to the surrounding countries. The Holy Land was a prize plum and much of her
history consists of her struggles to be free of the long invading arm of her neighbors.

To the south and west lay Egypt. In the days of the patriarchs—Abraham, Isaac and Jacob—Israel was a remote
province of the great Egyptian empire. There was much
travel to and from Egypt, mostly Hebrews who went as traders. Others were driven to Egypt by famine, like the brothers
of Joseph. In Egypt, the Hebrews came in contact with a
civilization much more advanced than their own. The Egyptians had already achieved the mighty engineering feat of the
Pyramids and the temples at Luxor and Karnak. The Hebrew visitors saw Egyptian art: delicately woven textiles,
hand-carved furniture, frescoes and jewelry. They undoubtedly came in contact with Egyptian picture-writing on papy-
rus. And when Moses led his people from slavery in Egypt,
his thoughts and teachings were naturally colored by the land
of his birth.

To the east were two great empires flourishing in the fertile area between the great rivers Tigris and Euphrates. They
were Babylon and, farther north, Assyria.

These kingdoms rose to power and fell away, but the course of their history is not germane to our subject. What is important is that these were mighty kingdoms: together with Egypt, the mightiest of their day. Their chief ambition was to strengthen their position by war and conquest, the Assyrians being the first people of the ancient world to learn the use of iron weapons.

The attitude of these great empires toward the Hebrews must have been much like that of the Japanese invaders toward the inhabitants of small South Pacific islands during the last war. Like those islands, the land of Israel was simply a small and insignificant steppingstone to greater things. Egypt, to the south, was the big objective. At one time the Assyrians extended their rule through the Holy Land and Egypt. In the process the Assyrian king, Sargon, destroyed the northern kingdom of the Hebrews (called Israel) and carried away part of its people as captives. After the center of Assyrian power moved to Babylon, Nebuchadnezzar, the Babylonian king, conquered the southern kingdom (called Judah) and took the best of its people into exile. This is the famous captivity of the Hebrews, which bulks so large in the mind of the Bible writers.

Here is part of Psalm 137, apparently written in captivity. It is certainly one of the saddest and most beautiful laments for one's native land that has ever been written. Although Zion refers specifically to the hill in Jerusalem on which the Temple stood, it is often used poetically, as here, to identify the entire land of the Hebrews:

By the rivers of Babylon,
There we sat down, yea, we wept,
When we remembered Zion.
We hanged our harps

Upon the willows in the midst thereof.
For there they that carried us away captive required of
    us a song,
And they that wasted us required of us mirth, saying,
"Sing us one of the songs of Zion."
How shall we sing the Lord's song
In a strange land?

If we look at the misfortunes of the Hebrews in the vast
scheme of history, we get a very different impression from
that conveyed by the Bible. Against this historical background the fortunes of Israel were insignificant. A highly
organized, culturally developed kingdom like Babylon over-
ran a minor nation. In point of the number of people involved, it was a small affair.

But spiritually the disasters of the Hebrews were of world-
shaking significance. For out of their tragedies the Hebrews
found a new understanding of the God it was their privilege
to love and serve. If Israel had not had a history full of disaster and triumph, she might not have had the food for
thought about God that led to so many new revelations of
his purpose and power. If the Hebrews had sat quietly in
the backwash of history, untouched by war, and death in war,
famine and slavery, they would never have faced the questions of human destiny that led them to such satisfying
answers. Their suffering, unjust and unending, helped them
discern God's method with men. It is this discernment which
speaks to us across the thousands of years and gives the
Bible its light.

The first sight of the Holy Land, situated at the far eastern
end of the Mediterranean is apt to bring a contradiction to
mind. How could a small country tucked in one corner of
the ancient world produce such an influential book? The

answer, as already pointed out, is not in the strength behind the book, but in the strength within it.

In fact, the Holy Land, first spoken of as Canaan, was about the same size as our state of Vermont, roughly 150 miles long, and at its widest point, 80 miles wide. A man could walk across a narrow part of the country from border to border, in just one day. When Joseph returned with Mary and Jesus from Egypt, it must have taken him about a week to arrive in Nazareth. When Jesus went from Nazareth, the scene of his boyhood, and traveled to Capernaum to begin his preaching, the trip probably took him five hours. The trip from the region of Galilee down to Jerusalem was about as far as from New York to Philadelphia, a walking trip of about three days.

The actual compass of Old and New Testament travels, then, is generally small. Think of living and traveling in the state of Vermont, for the truest feeling of space in most of the Bible story.

If in Bible times you could have climbed Mount Ebal, one of the centrally located peaks of the country, about three thousand feet in elevation, you would have been able to take in almost the whole expanse of Bible country just by sweeping your eyes in a circle around you.

To the west you would have seen the deep blue waters of the Mediterranean lapping the entire coastland from north to south, gleaming sand hills rising slightly from the sea and, behind them, a narrow, fertile lowland. To the south, this lowland bore the name of the Plain of Philistia. Its cities, Gaza, Gath, Ashkelon and Ashdod, all towns of the Philistines, are important in the stories of Samson and Saul. Just to the north of this plain, the lowland bore the name of the Plain of Sharon. The busy port city of Joppa was situated here, the city from which Jonah set sail, the city where Tabitha died and was recalled to life by Peter. Also on the plain of Sharon was the city of Caesarea, the official seat of the Herods, and the capital of Roman Palestine. Just to the north of the Plain of Sharon, the lowland is interrupted by Mount Carmel, scene of the great contest between Elijah and the prophets of Baal. Then the lowland continues as the Plain of Esdraelon, a vast arena in which many battles took place. Armies from the empires of Egypt, Assyria and Babylonia fought here. In the early days of the Bible, Barak and Gideon won their victories here. Saul was here defeated by the Philistines and Josiah by the Egyptians. Here the valiant Maccabees won freedom for the Hebrews. This plain is also said to be the Plain of Armageddon which the book of Revelation calls the place where "the kings of the earth and of the whole world" will gather for battle in the last days.

So much for the western view from your position atop Mount Ebal. Now turn your eyes northward. First you will see snow-crowned Mount Hermon, beyond the country's border, towering 9,000 feet above the sea. Then, at the northern point of the country, the city of Dan, and near it the important Roman town of Caesarea Philippi. Here Peter acknowledged the divinity of Jesus, and it marked the northern limit of Jesus' personal travels during his ministry.

The River Jordan intrudes upon your view now, the only river of any size in the land. It originates near Mt. Hermon, and about twenty miles below spreads out to form a beautiful lake. It is most commonly known as the Sea of Galilee, named after the fertile, well-watered and pleasant land of rolling hills, among which it nestles, although it is also called in the New Testament the Sea of Tiberias and the Lake of Gennesaret and, in the Old Testament, the Sea of Chinnereth.

Many of the famous places of the New Testament are located in the province of Galilee, including Nazareth, where Jesus grew to manhood. In the time of Jesus the province was a center of trade and transportation, located on a main highway of the Roman Empire. There were nine flourishing towns along the shores of the lake in those days. One of the nine was Capernaum, in whose synagogue Jesus preached, and near which it is believed he delivered the Sermon on the Mount. He lived in Peter's house in Capernaum and it was here that he met Matthew, a customs official at the quayside, and fishermen Simon and Andrew. Jesus spent much of his public life preaching here. Magdala, home of Mary Magdalene, was another city situated on the shores of the lake.

References to the Sea of Galilee abound in the New Testament. On these shores Jesus often walked. The region is quieter now than in his day, when it was crowded with shipping destined for the important port cities. Today's visitor sees only the town of Tiberias, founded by the Romans during Jesus' lifetime and mentioned only twice in the New Testament. The circle of cities whose handsome buildings were reflected in the calm blue mirror of the lake in Bible times have crumbled into ruin. Only the lake remains, still serene, still beautiful and still visited by sudden storms.

To the south, you see the province of Samaria. In fact, as you stand atop Mount Ebal you are in Samaria itself, for this is the central area. Its chief city, also called Samaria, was the seat of the northern kingdom (Israel) until it fell to the Assyrians in 722 B.C. The Old Testament sometimes refers to the kingdom of Israel as Samaria. Its inhabitants, the Samaritans are therefore both inhabitants of the city and of the kingdom. In New Testament times, the Samaritans were people with whom most of the other Jews had no dealings, because the Samaritans were of mixed blood and differed from the Jews in interpretation of religious matters. However,

Jesus in one of his most moving parables cast one Samaritan in a role which will guarantee these people a place in the world's memory. It is, of course, the story of the Good Samaritan, the compassionate traveler who helped the man wounded by thieves. The story is charged with even greater meaning when we realize the Samaritan's good-neighborliness was the act of an alien, a man who might easily have felt no compassion for his neighbors.

Still further south, beyond Samaria, you can see in the distance Judea, the rugged, mountainous southern province of the land. In the Old Testament, this was the land of Judah, where the southern kingdom, with its capital Jerusalem, thrived until 586 B.C. when Nebuchadnezzar took its people into captivity.

Two of the most meaningful events in the world's history took place in Judea, the birth and the death of Jesus. For "Joseph also went up from Galilee, out of the city of Nazareth, into Judea, unto the city of David, which is called Bethlehem . . ." and it was there that Mary "brought forth her firstborn son."

Jerusalem is just five miles north of Bethlehem. It is set on a rocky plateau, and when seen from the neighboring hills is still as the Bible describes it, "beautiful for situation, the joy of the whole earth." We can see how the physical setting of the Holy Land was often the raw material from which the Bible writers fashioned their words, by reading in Psalm 125:

> As the mountains are round about Jerusalem,
> So the Lord is round about his people
> From henceforth even forever.

Though the name Jerusalem may possibly mean "city of peace," it is a natural fortress, and has suffered many terrible sieges. When the Hebrews entered the promised land, the city was held by a Canaanite tribe. It was finally conquered by David, several centuries after the first invasion, and made into the capital of his kingdom. It reached its finest flowering under David's son Solomon, when the great Temple was built. It remained the capital of Judah, the southern kingdom, after it was separated from the northern kingdom.

Jerusalem is the most famous city in the Bible. There are countless references to it in both Testaments. It figured greatly in the thoughts of all the Hebrews. The psalmist writing of his homesickness in exile, sang,

> If I forget thee, O Jerusalem,
> Let my right hand forget her cunning.
> If I do not remember thee,
> Let my tongue cleave to the roof of my mouth;
> If I prefer not Jerusalem above my chief joy.

Jerusalem was the scene of many events in the ministry of Jesus, especially in the last days of his life.

The amazing Dead Sea lies to the south and east of Jerusalem. Thirteen hundred feet below sea level, it is so heavy with mineral salts that no living thing inhabits its waters and no vegetation can grow along its shores. Its extreme saltiness, five times greater than the ocean, is due to the rapid evaporation of its waters in the desert heat. The Jordan and many lesser streams empty into it but it has no outlet.

Turning now directly to the east, toward the great Syrian Desert, you will see the natural eastern boundary of the Holy Land running from north to south. It is the River Jordan. Originating on the slopes of Mount Hermon, it makes a rapid, crooked descent and empties into the Dead Sea. Several spots along the Jordan's banks as it passes near Jerusalem are pointed out as the scene of the baptism of Jesus by John the Baptist. In New Testament times as today most of the

Jordan Valley was a subtropical region with abundant verdure and a pleasant climate.

This brief eagle's-eye view of the land is intended only to sketch the major physical features. Remember that when reading the Bible, it is valuable to locate the events in your mind. A good map can be very helpful.

Think how this simple description of Jesus' travels becomes more real when you can picture his actual route: "He left Judea and departed again into Galilee. And he must needs go through Samaria." He was traveling from the barren, inhospitable province of Judea to the fertile north, and in so doing had to pass through Samaria, the central section.

When you know where men of the Bible fought, traveled, preached and prayed, you retain a living image of the life they lived. And so your reading becomes deeper and more rewarding.

Chapter 10

How History Helps You Understand the Bible

IT IS valuable to fix the main events of Hebrew history clearly in mind before taking up the Bible. Although the Bible presents its narrative of history in a fairly consecutive march, the great outlines of events are easily obscured by the countless, absorbing details in which they are clothed. The major events will tend to seem like pieces in an incomplete jigsaw puzzle, never quite fitting into an orderly pattern. The purpose of this chapter is to review very briefly the sweep of history as it is covered in the Bible: from about 2,000 B.C. down to the start of the Christian era.

This is also of help in reading the non-historical books of the Bible. For example, the later chapters of the book of Isaiah are best understood in light of the Babylonian exile. To profit from reading the prophet Jeremiah it is necessary to know at least the bare historical facts of the Assyrian and Babylonian invasions, predicted and participated in by Jeremiah. To understand the prophets Haggai and Zechariah, it is good to know what the situation was that greeted the Hebrews when they returned to their land from exile. And of course, knowing how the Romans came to be in Palestine in the lifetime of Jesus throws light on many events of his life, such as his famous words, "Render therefore unto Caesar the things which are Caesar's; and unto God the things that are God's," and the fact that he was brought before the Roman governor, Pontius Pilate.

The historical books of the Bible were not written as impartial, objective history, history as a modern historian would write it. There were already such books of strictly historical nature available when the Bible was being written, but since lost, such as *The History of the Kings of Judah* and *The History of the Kings of Israel,* and they are referred to in the Old Testament. No, our Bible histories are primarily religious books stressing that national prosperity depended upon loyalty to the Lord, and departure from God's law meant national disaster. The Jews to this day refer to several of these books not as books of history but as the "former Prophets."

But this fact should not tempt you to dismiss the historical sections of the Bible as mere legend. This would be as great an error as to take all of them as strictly historical records. The wisest course is to understand how the Bible writers saw and interpreted history. History for them was the action of the Lord, their God, in human affairs.

To appreciate this, it is necessary to know the secular history of the times; that is, the events as they would be seen by a modern historian. When this train of events is compared with the same events as described in the Bible, a clear understanding of the authors' working methods can be gained.

For example, in the first book of Kings, the Bible tells us that the Lord is angry at Solomon because he has been worshiping foreign gods. Solomon hears the Lord say, "Forasmuch as this is done of thee . . . I will surely rend the kingdom from thee and will give it to thy servant. Notwithstanding, in thy days I will not do it, for David thy father's sake: but I will rend it out of the hand of thy son. Howbeit I will not rend away all the kingdom; but will give one tribe to thy son for David my servant's sake, and for Jerusalem's sake which I have chosen."

Actual history shows us the Bible writer clearly at work. Facts reveal that Solomon ruled badly, in spite of his later reputation for wisdom. There was discontent over the high taxes he imposed to build his splendid buildings and the great Temple. His son, Rehoboam, ruled even more unwisely and a revolt deprived him of his kingdom—deprived him, that is, of all except the territory occupied by the tribe of Judah.

Now the writer of that passage in Kings knew that these events had come to pass. He was writing after they had occurred. But since his purpose was to explain all happenings in the light of divine intervention, we find him giving the Lord's annoyance with Solomon as the reason for the political changes. According to the writer's view of history, Solomon lost his kingdom because of his irreverence and disobedience, but because of the Lord's love of David, his father, the loss was postponed to the next generation and limited to part of the kingdom only. By rereading the passage quoted above, it becomes clear how each of the prophecies was fulfilled historically. In such a way the history writers of the Bible developed stories and proofs that God rewarded righteousness with prosperity and sin with misery and death.

Another habit of theirs was to omit historical facts which did not illuminate this thesis. For example, there was a king of northern Israel named Omri who reigned from about 887 to 875 B.C. From non-biblical sources we learn that he was one of the strongest monarchs the country ever had. He strengthened the nation and moved its capital to the hills of Samaria, where he fortified it so well that the Assyrians took three years to conquer it. He extended the kingdom to the east. He made treaties with his neighbors which proved profitable. For a hundred years after Omri, the Assyrian records refer to Israel as "the land of the house of Omri." Yet the Bible devotes only six verses to this king, who from our viewpoint as readers of history would seem worth a chapter or two. For any reader of the book of Kings who wanted the rest of the story, the record says (I Kings, Chapter 16), "Now the rest of the acts of Omri which he did, and his might that he showed, are they not written in the book of the chronicles of the Kings of Israel?" Those are the secular historical books already referred to, which have since been lost. Omri's deeds were considered relevant to those works, but not appropriate for our book of I Kings because they did not underscore the thesis that God dealt with people according to the way they dealt with him. For the events seemed to contradict the design: Israel prospered under Omri even though he did not observe the Lord's law properly.

I. THE DAWN OF HEBREW HISTORY (From earliest times to about 1250 B.C.)

The first Hebrews drifted into the land that was to become their home somewhere around the twentieth century, B.C. The actual time and details are lost in legend for us. We have only the Bible's account of these days, no records from other sources to confirm or deny what the sacred text tells us. The Bible says that Abraham led the loosely joined clans forming the Hebrew tribe out of the Tigris-Euphrates valley and toward the Mediterranean. This trek from east to west was about the distance from Chicago to Denver. Like our Pilgrim Fathers, Abraham was in search of freedom; in this case, freedom to worship the one God who had spoken to him, promising that his descendants would become a great people.

The men and women of this dawn of history, Abraham and

his wife Sarah, Isaac and his wife Rebekah and his sons Esau and Jacob, are in effect the founders of the Hebrew nation. Their story, written centuries later by men who had heard only dim legends of their activities, reveal them as people with a strong sense of family and clan, quick-thinking, adaptable, full of imagination, and above all, worshipers of one God instead of many.

We know that they did not find the land of Canaan, as their site of settlement was called, uninhabited. It had been occupied for centuries by a mixture of tribes known as Canaanites. There was constant friction between the early Hebrew settlers and these natives.

The book of Genesis, which describes the lives of these patriarchs (as they are called) contains many of the best-known tales of the Old Testament. Here we meet Sarah, who conceived her son Isaac in her old age; we hear of Abraham's willingness to sacrifice his son Isaac at God's command; we read of the wooing of Rebekah by Isaac and of the contest of their two sons, Esau and Jacob, for their father's precious blessing.

Jacob, Abraham's grandson, had twelve sons who are cited as the founders of the twelve tribes of Israel, of whom we hear all through the Old Testament. Jacob himself was also referred to as Israel, meaning "God persists" or "God contends" or "God does battle," a name which has distinguished the Hebrew people from all others ever since, and is now the name of the new Hebrew state in Palestine.

In these days the Hebrews had no settled homes, but wandered from place to place in search of water and pasture. They stayed in one spot only as long as the pasture lasted. Their needs and belongings were scanty. Their homes were tents made of cloth woven from goats' hair.

Apparently fortune smiled on the newcomers from the

east. They saw their herds multiply and their families increase. Because of this, in time their herdsmen began to
quarrel about grazing boundaries and rights to springs and
streams. So they agreed to separate. This has often been the
reason why nomadic peoples separate into different clans and
tribes.

Did the Hebrew nomads believe in human sacrifice, as did
many ancient peoples? Not after Abraham's time. The end
of this cruel custom is made clear in the exciting tale of the
near-sacrifice of Isaac.

What were their marriage customs? All of literature does
not offer more beautiful and revealing stories than those of
Isaac and his wooing of Rebekah, and how Jacob was tricked
by his sly father-in-law into working fourteen years for the
girl he loved.

A great change occurred when the Hebrew nomads left
the land of Canaan and went south to Egypt. This may have
been because of famine, as the Bible says. Probably only a
few thousand people were involved in the transfer, and apparently they were free in Egypt to keep their customs and
way of worship.

The Bible clothes this great historical change in the unforgettable story of Joseph the firstborn son of Jacob's second,
and most beloved, wife, Rachel. How Joseph, the spoiled
darling of his parents, aroused the jealousy of his older brothers who sold him into slavery in Egypt opens one of the
world's most drama-packed stories.

II. THE BIRTH OF A NATION (From the Exodus, about
    1250 B.C. to the founding of the Kingdom, about 1030
    B.C.)

Most historians today accept as historical fact the Bible's
statement that part, at least, of the Hebrews lived in Egypt.

Inscriptions found on ancient Egyptian monuments can be interpreted as a reference to them. Again, we must winnow from the Bible the bare historical facts of their sojourn there, since the Bible is our only sourcebook of the times.

In the course of time, at least several generations after their arrival in Egypt, the Hebrews fell out of favor with the rulers of the land. As the Bible puts it, "there arose up a new king over Egypt, which knew not Joseph." We can surmise that the new king was afraid the foreigners would become too powerful or numerous and possibly develop into a revolutionary party. To forestall this, he began to persecute the Hebrews. How long they were forced to work under slave conditions as makers and layers of brick we cannot know, but gradually the time grew ripe for their deliverance under Moses.

The background of the story changes with the last verse of the first chapter of Exodus. Behind the story of the Hebrew people from this moment onward stands Moses. Historically speaking, Moses must be considered one of the great figures of world history. His achievements were gigantic, measured by any standards. He must have been a man of towering personality, both leader and teacher. Whatever one's interpretation of the plagues which scourged the Egyptians and helped Moses free his people, it must be admitted that this one man's energy and force played a vital part in his success. He led the fight for freedom.

Moses molded the loose collection of family groups into a people with a mission. The Hebrews had gone into Egypt as a scattering of families with some customs and observances in common: language, marriage, religion. By the time they re-entered the land of Canaan, the promised land, they were a united political group with a new sense of their identity and destiny.

This great change came about mostly through the giving of the Ten Commandments to Moses, on the way to Canaan. It was from this Mosaic code, a unifying body of laws, that the great consensus of Hebrew legislation was to spring. It was from this code that the Hebrews were inspired with a much clearer idea of their relationship to God and to each other. The nation whose fate is the concern of the Bible was born as a political unit on the dark night when Moses called upon his children to rise up.

The escaping Hebrews passed many years in the wilderness between Egypt and the land the Lord had promised Moses. Their struggles with hunger and thirst and their questionings about the God that had brought them out of Egypt—doubts resolved by Moses' force of personality—helped to forge a stronger national character. These difficult years helped them grow in faith, both in God and in law and order. Moses, the Bible tells us, did not live to enter Canaan. However, he saw it with his own eyes from the top of the mountain called Pisgah. It was the work of his people to subdue that land and make it sustain them.

Let us try to get an idea of the conquest of Canaan from a historical point of view. Again, this means sifting down the Bible description of it to surmise what actually happened, to look behind the religious interpretation put on the events by the Bible writers. These days of conquest are reflected in the books of Joshua and Judges and the first book of Samuel.

First, we must not think of the Hebrew invaders as a vast army of people. They were still in small tribal groups, completely unlike the organized armies of the Persians or Romans. They were few in number, no more than several thousand men, women and children. And they did not attack as an army. More likely, they won minor skirmishes here and there: one tribe against a town or district of Canaan. Undoubtedly their weapons were not as good as those of the men they fought.

If all these military deficiencies were true, and we can assume they were, what was the secret of their success? The explanation lies in a factor known to every general who ever led an army. Today we call it morale. The morale of the Hebrews must have been magnificent, and traceable directly to their belief, never to be denied, that their God was a God of battles and that he had promised them the victory. They might forget their God in times of peace when all was going well; later they often did. But in time of battle the Hebrews believed with all their hearts that God was on their side, helping them prevail over their enemies. No Canaanite village, no matter how well defended, could long hold out against these fierce and dedicated warriors, unshakably inspired with the belief that they were the armies of the Lord.

As pointed out before, Canaan was only the size of Vermont. The country's towns and strongholds were small too; probably no more than 1,500 people lived in a sizable Canaanite town. Nevertheless, the conquest of Canaan was not easy. It took at least two centuries of almost constant battling before the land was subdued.

III. THE MINIATURE KINGDOMS (From about 1030 B.C. to 586 B.C.)

At about the same time that the Hebrews were pressing their conquest of Canaan from the east, a people called in the Bible Philistines were securing a foothold in the west. They were a seafaring people and had established themselves in a group of city-states along the coastal plain in southwest Canaan. Their cities were Gaza, Gath, Ekron, Ashkelon and Ashdod. They were skilled warriors, with a native talent for military organization and action. Their forcefulness is reflected in the fact that the word Palestine, derived from their name, clung to this region for centuries after their own disappearance. The Philistines won easily in their early battles with the Israelite tribes in the hill country just above the coast. In one disastrous encounter they added insult to injury by carrying off the sacred Ark of the Lord, a chest containing the two tablets of stone with the Ten Commandments engraved on them which invariably accompanied the Hebrews in their campaigns.

This catastrophe provoked certain beneficial events. In effect, it marked a turning point in Hebrew history. It proved that a new form of government was essential, one that could prepare the nation for unified battle against a powerful enemy, unlike the disorganized Canaanites. From the time of their entry into the new land, the Hebrews had been ruled by judges, local strongmen, roughly comparable to the feudal lords of Europe's Middle Ages. There was no central government. But now it became clear that all must unite or be destroyed piecemeal by the marauding Philistines.

A highly respected wise man, or seer, Samuel, chose a man named Saul to be the first king and anointed him. Saul faced problems of the first magnitude. Because the nation was newly a kingdom, his throne was not secure. At first he was little more than another tribal judge. But in the early years of his reign, he won some successful campaigns against the Philistines, which helped him gain acceptance for the throne. Before long, however, he fell out with Samuel, the seer who had anointed him, and his power and popularity began to wane.

For at least ten of the twenty years of his rule, Saul's life was marred by his passionate jealousy and hatred of David, his former friend. As time passed, David grew in stature and popularity. Saul plotted David's death, unsuccessfully, and finally went insane and fell on his own sword in battle.

After Saul's death, David proved himself to be a master of diplomacy and strategy. With the help of his country's enemies, the Philistines (and this amounted to near treason) he defended himself against Abner, the captain of Saul's army and against the king's weak son who had succeeded him. In the drawn-out feud between the houses of David and Saul, David became more and more popular. Finally, about the year 1000 B.C., David was acknowledged king of all Israel. One of the first things he did was to capture a hitherto impregnable fortress in the very heart of Canaan, called Jebus. This he renamed Jerusalem and made his capital. The "City of David" as Jerusalem has been called, in time acquired great religious and emotional meaning for the Hebrews.

David made Jerusalem a national shrine, bringing there the sacred Ark after retrieving it from the Philistines. This is one of the most vivid moments in the Old Testament: "And David and all the house of Israel played before the Lord on all manner of instruments made of fir wood, even on harps, and on psalteries and on timbrels, and on cornets, and on cymbals." As the Ark of the Lord came into the city of David, the Bible says the king was "leaping and dancing before the Lord."

David erected great walls around Jerusalem and built a royal palace. He was Israel's greatest warrior. After beating the Philistines and reducing them to vassalage, he conquered in turn the other nations round about, until he had established a miniature empire extending from the river Euphrates on the northeast to the Gulf of Akaba (Red Sea) on the south. As long as David lived, his subject states did not revolt against him. His reign marked the fullest political flowering of the Hebrew people. It is referred to again and again later in the Bible, since it lived on always in their hearts as a symbol of earthly success.

David raised the Hebrew people from insignificance on the world stage to a minor glory. The Bible gives us some information about the elaborate organization he built. Translated into modern terms we find references to a prime minister, a secretary of state, a king's chaplain, a secretary of the treasury, a collector of vineyard revenue, a collector of oil revenue, a secretary of agriculture, sheep inspectors and camel inspectors. David made his nation the most important state between the old and powerful empires of Egypt and Assyria. This is why he was considered the perfect king and why the tradition grew that the Messiah, or Deliverer, would be born of his house. The story of David's reign is told in the two books of Samuel and in the first book of Kings; also in the first book of Chronicles.

At the time of Saul's investiture as king, each of the twelve tribes consisting traditionally of the descendants of Jacob's twelve sons, settled in an agreed-upon portion of the promised land. By David's reign their transformation from wanderers to farmers had become complete. No longer did they drift from camp to camp, without fixed homes and hearths and fields. They became cultivators of land, growers of grain, grapes, olives and figs. They became an established people, thrusting emotional roots into the land and building communities.

The difference was tremendous and is mirrored in the Bible. References to vineyards, corn, figs, olives suddenly abound. Instead of bringing only young animals for religious offerings, they brought the first fruits of the land, doves and pigeons.

In the New Testament, Jesus refers to "Solomon in all his glory." No single phrase could describe Solomon's reign more accurately. He glamorized what his father David had bequeathed him. His regal interest was in consolidation and aggrandizement. He spared no expense in his building program in Jerusalem, the main feature of which was the Temple described in detail in the fifth and sixth chapters of the first book of Kings. His industrial and commercial enterprises sound almost modern to us. He established a merchant marine at the head of one of the arms of the Red Sea. On the highway to his chief port he developed copper and iron mines, the famous "King Solomon's mines." Recent archaeology has revealed him to have been both a merchant prince and industrial magnate.

All these enterprises, plus his extensive harem (reportedly seven hundred wives and three hundred concubines), created a heavy tax burden which was to cause his eventual downfall. His people were required to pay taxes not only in cash but in labor. Never popular anywhere at any time, such measures were fiercely resented by the Hebrews.

The opposition organized and found a champion, a priest named Ahijah. He picked as the man to head the revolt the superintendent of the forced labor gangs, Jeroboam. The plot was to have the ten northern tribes, which had never been completely unified with the two southern tribes of Judah and Benjamin, secede from the union. The plot was nipped in the bud and Jeroboam escaped to Egypt, to be heard from later.

King Solomon died in the year 931 B.C. His son Rehoboam undoubtedly took it for granted that he would become king over a unified kingdom. But the northern tribes (hereafter always spoken of as Israel in contrast to the southern as Judah) had their tax grievances to settle first. The elders of Israel met at Shechem. The story of their deliberations is one of the great pronouncements of history where men are free to express themselves. It declares that a ruler is not an overlord, but the servant of the people.

However, Rehoboam refused to lighten their yoke and they revolted, successfully. The kingdom was cut in half, never to be joined again.

Jeroboam, who had led the abortive revolt during Solomon's reign, returned from exile to become the first king of northern Israel. The Bible says, with typical brevity, "and there was war between Rehoboam and Jeroboam perpetually." In fact it continued for fifty years, running far beyond the reigns of the two kings who began it.

Following the division of the Hebrew kingdom in 931 B.C., both Israel and Judah began a process of deterioration. We cannot follow their complicated history in this brief space, but for two centuries each continued under its own rulers, some good, some bad. The books of Kings and Chronicles record the history of this period. It was in these troubled days that the greatest of the prophets appeared: Amos, Isaiah, Micah and Jeremiah, of whom we shall speak in detail later.

As time passed and the various kings described in the Old Testament came and went, the Hebrews remained chiefly an agricultural people. However, their cities grew in size, and the more adventurous among them started to trade with neighboring people of other faiths.

The presence of pagans on all sides, men and women who did not believe in the overruling Lord Jehovah, had always presented many problems of faith to the Hebrews. Many of the gods worshipped by surrounding people were purely fertility gods: they had a definite economic value because the proper worship of them could supposedly increase the size of herds and the yield of crops. The pressure on the Hebrews to put their faith in these gods too was great. The prophets, men with the self-appointed task of making their people hold to the strict line of their faith, were always protesting against this tendency. The fertility cults of Baal and Ashtoreth seem to have been the main temptations. The most dramatic of these protests is in the clash of Elijah with the prophets of Baal related in the eighteenth chapter of the first book of Kings. Elijah staged a contest with the priests of the heathen gods, and emerged the victor.

Israel, the northern kingdom, met its doom almost one hundred and fifty years before the southern kingdom of Judah. It was overrun by the Assyrians in 721 B.C. and its inhabitants scattered throughout the Assyrian empire. These ten tribes dispersed by the Assyrians are the famous "lost tribes of Israel" of whom no trace has ever been uncovered.

For Judah, the southern kingdom, the story is quite different. She survived principally because of the tribute she paid to Assyria. Judah had one hairbreadth's escape from the Assyrians. In 701 B.C., just twenty years after the Assyrians had demolished the northern kingdom, they returned under their leader, Sennacherib, and camped outside the walls of Jerusalem. At this moment, the prophet Isaiah, alone among the Hebrews, had faith in the continued freedom of his country. His stirring words to his country's king still sound a thrilling note: "Therefore thus saith the Lord concerning the king of Assyria, 'He shall not come into this city, nor shoot an arrow there, nor come before it with shield, nor cast a bank against it. By the way that he came, by the same shall he return, and shall not come into this city,' saith the Lord. 'For I will defend this city to save it, for mine own sake, and for my servant David's sake.'"

Isaiah spoke truly, for as the Bible says, "It came to pass

that night, that the angel of the Lord went out, and smote in the camp of the Assyrians an hundred fourscore and five thousand: and when they arose early in the morning, behold, they were all dead corpses."

Some modern historians believe that a sudden outbreak of plague in the Assyrian camp caused the many deaths. Lord Byron dramatized the Bible's version of the event in one of his most beautiful poems, "The Destruction of Sennacherib":

> The Assyrian came down like a wolf on the fold,
> And his cohorts were gleaming in purple and gold;
> And the sheen of their spears was like stars on the sea,
> When the blue wave rolls nightly on deep Galilee.
>
> Like the leaves of the forest when Summer is green,
> That host with their banners at sunset were seen:
> Like the leaves of the forest when Autumn hath blown,
> That host on the morrow lay withered and strown.
>
> For the Angel of Death spread his wings on the blast,
> And breathed in the face of the foe as he passed;
> And the eyes of the sleepers waxed deadly and chill,
> And their hearts but once heaved, and forever grew still! . . .
>
> And the widows of Ashur are loud in their wail,
> And the idols are broke in the temple of Baal;
> And the might of the Gentile, unsmote by the sword,
> Hath melted like snow in the glance of the Lord!

After this episode the Assyrian star began to decline and Judah enjoyed relative peace for a time, though still a vassal state. Assyria's mantle of conquest was assumed by the Babylonians, who were soon to visit the little land.

Jeremiah was now the great prophet. He called for an end to the worship of the foreign gods which had infiltrated the country. He predicted the doom of the nation unless it returned to the true worship of Jehovah. Jeremiah's powerful preaching sparked a wave of reform in Judah under the direction of King Josiah who reigned from 639 B.C. to 609 B.C.

The Temple, which had fallen into disrepair during seventy-five years of use in the worship of foreign gods, was now restored. In the process of repairing it, a scroll was discovered which contained an interpretation of the old laws of the nation, the ancient religious and moral laws first promulgated by Moses. This dramatic incident, which must have seemed God-inspired to the men and women of Jerusalem, also served to highlight the difference between the behavior of the day and the former practices of the Hebrews. The king, Josiah, was so stirred by this that he held a national assembly at the Temple, at which a solemn agreement was made that this law would in future be the basis of the nation's life. The book found in the Temple at this time is generally believed to be the basis for our book of Deuteronomy. The word "Deuteronomy" is Greek for "the second giving of the law."

Unfortunately, Josiah's reforms were short-lived. He was followed by less wise monarchs, who failed to unite and inspire their threatened country. The king of Babylon, Nebuchadnezzar, invaded the country, laid siege to Jerusalem and subdued it in 597 B.C. Its most important citizens were carried into exile. Eleven years later, in 586 B.C., he returned and destroyed the city entirely, carrying many more Hebrews into captivity. So Judah shared the fate of its twin kingdom, Israel, the last remnant of David's empire was destroyed, and the bitter fifty-year exile by the rivers of Babylon began.

IV. THE CAPTIVITY IN BABYLON (586-536 B.C.)

Although the Hebrew exiles in Babylon were captives, they were not jailed and guarded. On the contrary, they were free to come and go as they pleased, within limits.

They were kept together in a group, not scattered across

the empire as their unfortunate countrymen had been one hundred and fifty years before. If they had been scattered, they could not have survived as a national and religious group; instead of ten lost tribes there would have been twelve. And we would have no Bible today. But Nebuchadnezzar, the king, was generous (or uninterested) enough to keep his involuntary guests together, along the canals which crisscrossed lower Babylonia.

The Hebrews saw things in the land of exile which they probably had never dreamed possible. The fertile soil permitted productive farming, more productive than the rocky soil of Palestine. Here they could raise enough to eat, with some left over to sell. They could become fairly prosperous farmers, no longer struggling for a bare livelihood from unresponsive soil.

Babylon was also a great commercial center. Many Hebrews quit farming for commerce and probably it was during these years that the process began which has made the Jews into the world's traders.

What about their religious life? Fortunately, they were allowed to practice their religion without hindrance. They were free to worship their God. Of course there were some, in the face of new financial prosperity and fading memories of home, who were weaned away from the Lord. They began to worship the gods of the Babylonians. It was the same backsliding the prophets had railed against at home, this time based on the rationalization that if Jehovah had sent them into exile and Bel-Marduk, the god of Babylon, had made them prosperous, why not worship Bel?

But many more clung to the old worship and to the thoughts of the land they had left. Although they had no temple in which to worship, they could still meet together and talk about God and his commandments. They could comfort one another. They could pray and sing the songs of Zion.

Under these circumstances, a change began to take place in Jewish religious life. They discovered that the inner force and ethical vitality of their religion was just as powerful as ever. They discovered that their idea of God was not tied to any one place; it was as valid in Babylon as in the land where it had emerged. Two major developments came from this discovery.

One was the rise of the synagogue, a local institution for worship. We find this mentioned frequently in the New Testament, and it was to become the model for the Christian church, whose places of worship sprang up everywhere. The other was the opportunity to collect and study the sermons of the prophets and the nation's historical records, which resulted in the gradual collection and editing of those documents which together became the Old Testament. The editors must have felt that since the ideas could live in Babylon, they could also live in written form. This was the next step in freeing their ideas from the narrow concept of locality. Manuscripts, a portable fatherland for the Hebrews, were beginning to take form. A new responsibility was felt: to select, edit and preserve the writings which best reflected their finest thoughts. The Bible was beginning.

Nebuchadnezzar's kingdom crumbled only twenty-two years after his death, when it was merged into the much larger empire of Cyrus, a Persian king. Cyrus had a different idea of how to rule his conquered nations: he believed in courting their loyalty. So in the year 538 B.C., he bestowed freedom on the exiled Jews and gave them permission to travel back to their fatherland. A year later the first group turned their faces westward to the land from which they or their fathers had come.

Except for certain hints in Ezra and Nehemiah, the years of the exile are not described in any of the historical books of the Bible. There is no attempt to narrate the events in their order. Instead we find the exile *reflected* in the writings of the prophet Ezekiel, in the book of Isaiah from the fortieth chapter on, and in some of the Psalms.

V. THE TROUBLED YEARS OF THE RETURN (536-320 B.C.)

Of course, not all the exiled Hebrews returned. A half century brings many changes. A new generation had grown up who knew of Jerusalem only through the tales of their fathers. Their roots were in Babylon, where their business and social interests were. Only the older people, and by no means all of them, had any desire to return. It involved danger and hardship, with little hope of immediate success.

And what they found in their homeland confirmed their worst fears. Jerusalem was a place of desolation. Its walls had been razed and its buildings were in ruins. The Temple on Mount Zion was gone. Untended orchards and vineyards were overrun with weeds and briars. Many villages and towns, fired by the marauding Babylonians, had been abandoned, and been overgrown by grass in fifty desolate years.

But that was not all. Some of the neighboring peoples, Ammonites and Samaritans and Edomites, had moved in on the partially depopulated country and taken possession. Some of them had married with the Hebrews left behind. The returning Hebrews, their sense of apartness made stronger than ever, were horrified to see these strangers within their gates. We find this condition reflected in the books of the prophets Haggai and Zechariah, with their concern over intermarriage.

It was around this time that the feeling against Samaritans

was born. In contrast to the practice of the more orthodox Jews, some members of the colony had intermarried with the Babylonians during the captivity and still others with the people of Canaan when they returned. These resettlers of mixed blood were never acceptable to the strict observers of the law, and were called Samaritans. They built a small temple of their own in the city of Shechem about twenty-five miles north of Jerusalem. The distinction between Jews and Samaritans exists to this day.

The first years of the return were anything but successful. Crops were bad, neighbors became increasingly hostile against the exclusiveness of the Jews, and the time, energy and money to rebuild the Temple and the walls could not be found. But gradually as more time passed, new forces began to stir. The encouragements of the prophets Haggai and Zechariah brought about the rebuilding of the Temple, in 520 B.C., sixteen years after the return. The Temple was finished four years later, in 516 B.C. This meant that although the Hebrew community had no political existence, that is, was not self-governing, but merely a province of the Persian empire, ruled by a foreign governor, it had at least re-established the religious observances which had been the basis of national unity for many centuries.

In the century which followed, the country was still under Persian rule, but Hebrew leaders arose who welded their people into a stronger, more optimistic group, always with their religion as the basis for their unity. One of these leaders was Ezra, reputedly a "scribe skilled in the law of Moses" who is chiefly credited with re-establishing strict temple worship. The other was Nehemiah, probably the most energetic character in the Old Testament. He brought new life and strength to the community when he arrived in Jerusalem in the year 444 B.C. He had been a Hebrew in the service of

Artaxerxes, the Persian emperor, and had won permission to return to his native land as governor to see to its rebuilding. The book which bears his name bears witness to his energy. Thanks mainly to his efforts the walls of Jerusalem were rebuilt in only fifty-two days, the men working "from the rising of the morning till the stars appeared." Nehemiah forbade mixed marriages, reinstated respect for the Sabbath, proclaimed assemblies and in general brought back to life the languishing Jewish community. In place of the vanished kingdoms and sovereign peoples of the old days, he set up a religious state, governed almost completely by the high priest and held together by that complicated but inspiring body of laws, teachings and customs known to us today as Judaism.

We know little about the Jewish community from the time of Nehemiah until the conquest by Alexander about a century later. The great racial and religious exclusiveness of the Hebrews isolated them from the outside world, even from the doings of the rest of the Persian empire. The lines of trade and traffic which had linked them to the outer world seem to have been broken in these post-exilic times.

In 332 B.C. Alexander the Great conquered the Persians and became the new master of the little Bible land. Its occupation was just one phase, and to his generals probably a very unimportant one, of his mighty march of conquest from west to east. Before his sudden death only nine years later, his empire stretched from Greece as far as India.

Alexander was more than a world conqueror. He was a world civilizer. Everywhere he went in the Orient he brought Greek ways, Greek learning, Greek habits. The fusion of Greek (or Hellenic) culture with Oriental cultures produced what is known as Hellenism.

Among the great cities which Alexander planted was one

at the northwest apex of the Nile delta in Egypt. He named
it after himself, Alexandria. By allocating a section of the
city to the Jews, he stimulated migration there, and here the
Jews established a great center of learning.

The Jews in the Holy Land fiercely resented Greek ways,
just as they had always resented and resisted the way of any
alien group. They clung to their high priest as their true
ruler and to the Aramaic language, which had been the
tongue of the Persian empire.

A word here about the dispersion of the Jews across the
Mediterranean world. During all the political upheavals
that marked the last centuries of the Old Testament story,
countless Hebrews fled their country. They went not only
for political reasons, to escape the vengeance of the Babylonians, but also for economic reasons. Their native country
was small, its land poor; as time passed the pressure of over-
crowding became great. Many families had to find homes
in other countries simply because their own was not large
enough to support them. Usually they found only foreign
cities were hospitable; the land itself was jealously guarded
by natives. This meant that most of them became tradesmen
and merchants. By the time of the New Testament we find
colonies of Hebrews in every major section of the Roman
Empire.

VI. THE TIMES OF SUBJECTION (323 B.C. to the Chris-
tian era)

When Alexander died in 323, his empire was divided
among his generals. Egypt, with the Holy Land, fell to Ptolemy. It remained the possession of the Ptolemaic dynasty,
the successors of Ptolemy, until 198 B.C., when it was wrested
away by the descendants of another of Alexander's generals.

This was the Syrian king, Antiochus III, whose capital was directly north of the Holy Land, in Antioch.

When the land became subject to this king, things began to go badly for the Jews. Antiochus was determined that the Hellenizing process should be applied thoroughly. His grandson, Antiochus Epiphanes, carried these ideas to the limit, demanding that even the Jewish religion be Hellenized. He demanded that they abandon their worship and serve the Greek deities, Zeus, Aphrodite, Hera and the rest. He renamed the Temple after the Greek god, Zeus. Finally came the fateful day in 168 B.C. when a pig was offered in sacrifice on the altar in the great Temple itself. Virtually nothing on earth could have been more sacrilegious to orthodox Jews. The era of unspeakable persecution which followed is the reason why the author of the book of Daniel wrote in allegory. He could not name the names of persecutors or deeds of persecution. So he clothed his narrative in symbols and hidden meanings.

At this point, a little village about seventeen miles northwest of Jerusalem becomes the center of Hebrew history. It was called Modin and among its villagers was an old priest, Mattathias. When the king's emissaries arrived at Modin to compel the sacrifice of swine on the village altar, Mattathias not only refused to perform the rite, but when he saw a collaborating Jew step forth to do it he killed both the Jew and the king's emissary. Then he tore down the altar and called upon all loyal men to rally to his cause.

Mattathias had five sons, of whom one, named Judas Maccabeus, became the leader of the cause his father had taken up. Judas Maccabeus (his last name means The Hammerer) conquered four Syrian armies sent against him the following two years. A fifth was forced to retire. This great chapter in Jewish history is written down in the first book of the Maccabees, which is unfortunately not included in the standard Protestant Bible. It will be found, however, in all Catholic Bibles and such other editions as include the apocryphal books.

Judas took his victorious army to Jerusalem, where he removed the desecrated altar, and built a new one; and in the year 165 B.C., around the twenty-fifth of December, began a happy feast of rededication that lasted eight days. This feast is still celebrated every year by Jews, and is known as the feast of Chanukkah or the Festival of Lights.

Judas Maccabeus won religious liberty for his people, and by the year 143 B.C. had won their political liberty also. The little country was completely independent once again—for the first time in more than four hundred years. It was a proud moment in its history.

Unfortunately, this independence was of short duration. A series of unwise rulers and bitter strife between elements in the population led to weakness. Finally, the priestly party appealed to Rome for help. By this time, Rome had become the dominant ruler of the world, and was the symbol of law and order to nations who could not rule themselves without wrangling. The priests asked Pompey, the Roman leader, to recognize neither of the parties then warring for control, but to restore the former type of government, rule by high priests and senate. Pompey used this as an excuse to enter the country. In the year 63 B.C., he besieged Jerusalem. After three months of blood-soaked resistance by the Jews holding the citadel and the Temple, the mailed legions of Rome entered the ancient city. So began Rome's seven-century grip on the country followed by more centuries of rule by other powerful neighbors. Not until A.D. 1948 did it again come under Jewish self-rule.

The land we meet in the New Testament was a Roman

province, with no shadow of political freedom. Over sixty years had passed since the first Roman order was shouted within earshot of the faithful who came to worship at the Temple. The flaming ardor of the Maccabees and their revolt had cooled down to mere restlessness. The cause was lost, the hope of unity abandoned, the chance of an earthly kingdom whose majesty might rival the vanished empire of David no longer dreamed of. This is the state of the Hebrews we meet in the New Testament—a people with no government of their own, completely controlled by Roman governors. A bitter situation for a fierce, proud, independent people still secretly possessed by the idea that their God had singled them out above all other people of the earth.

Small wonder, then, that their anger and hate, powerless to harm the imperturbable Romans, made them turn on each other in endless, bitter arguing. The population of Jerusalem, the seething pot of Hebrew discontent, was split into opposing groups, some political, some religious.

There were the Herodians, taking their name from the last line of the Hebrew puppet kings whom we find in power at the opening of the New Testament but who were later replaced by a Roman governor. The Herodians were full of Greek thoughts and ways, ready to drop the time-honored Jewish customs for more modern ideas.

There were the Zealots, patriots plotting to throw off the Roman yoke, but without success.

There were the Pharisees, a New Testament term so common that we have an unlovely English adjective derived from it. To many Bible readers this name brings up the image of bitter, sectarian men who denounced Christ when he preached his new humanitarian ideas. But the Pharisees were not always so. When the order was founded, just before the Maccabean revolt, it was inspired by high motives, unselfish patriotism and faith in God. But as time went by, the Pharisees became a meddlesome sect, devoted to the letter, but not the spirit, of the ancient laws. They failed to keep up with the times. They turned their back on the living present and declared that only by adhering to every last detail in the old texts—and to many special regulations of their own—could one be righteous.

There were the Sadducees, also familiar to New Testament readers. They were usually wealthy men, with a vested interest in seeing that the order of things was not upset.

When the Pharisees denounced Jesus because of his unorthodox ideas of religion, the Sadducees joined in because Jesus seemed to be a menace to law and order. The Pharisees feared his doctrines, but the Sadducees feared the political effect of his doctrines. The court before which Jesus was tried was the Sanhedrin, presided over by the high priest and composed of both Sadducees and Pharisees. The Sanhedrin judged Jesus to be worthy of death for blasphemy, but did not have the authority to pass sentence. This the Roman governor, Pontius Pilate, had to do. The technical charge was treason, because Jesus had called himself King of the Jews. But the underlying reason was the fear of the Pharisees and Sadducees that Jesus would upset the religious and political order. So he was condemned to die by crucifixion.

This was the end of another bloody episode in the life of the Jewish people, or so thought the men who were responsible for the tragic deed. But because it was not the end we have the New Testament and the whole world has the Bible.

Chapter 11

The Men of Mighty Words

AT THE close of Paul's second letter to the congregation of Thessalonica, he writes, "I, Paul, write this greeting with my own hand. This is the mark in every letter of mine; it is the way I write. The grace of our Lord Jesus Christ be with you all."

Paul had apparently taken the stylus from the hand of the professional writer to whom he had been dictating, in order to end his letter with these words. As he says, he did this at the close of every letter.

As he finishes his letter to the Galatians, he makes a similar comment. He says, "See with what large letters I am writing to you with my own hand." We can guess that his scrawling penmanship was in bold contrast to the neat writing of the professional.

We quote these remarks of Paul because they are so exceptional. For the most part, we have only vague ideas about the identities of the men who wrote the Bible. Most books, unlike Paul's letters, are not signed.

This is understandable for several reasons. In the days when the words were being written which would later be incorporated into the Bible, very few people could write. Whatever words were written were treasured and guarded and easily traceable back to their author. No author need stamp his name on his work; the few who could read would know its origin anyway.

Another reason for the anonymity of the Bible books is the fact that so many people were involved in shaping them as they finally came to us. Besides the original writers, there were often later copyists and still later editors. All these added their mite to the text, until each section became a mosaic of different men's work. Only in a few cases, as we shall see, did one man compose a whole book. Especially in the case of the historical books and the anthologies like Psalms and Proverbs, many men contributed.

The last reason for this state of affairs goes deeper. The Bible writers had only one purpose in setting down their words: they wanted to give longer life and wider circulation to their religious ideas. They wanted to publish their faith in God, in words that would not fade easily from memory. They wrote not to express themselves but to express God and that is a crucial distinction. What were their own names when compared to the name of the Lord? Much better to remain nameless and faceless, submerged in the larger identity of Jehovah, their God.

Let us take a quick look at the thoughts of recent scholars on the authorship of some of the books which comprise the Old Testament. As already pointed out, these books were written over a period of possibly two thousand years. Except for brief parts of several of the books written last, all were set down in the Hebrew language.

First we must become familiar with the traditional Hebrew arrangement of the books comprising the Old Testament. In Part I of the present book, we arranged the books of the Old Testament according to subject matter into three large categories: historical writing, prophetical writing and sacred literature (the latter including poems, a drama, biographical sketches and philosophy). This is a convenient and logical way to classify the books in our own mind. However, the Hebrews divided the books into three categories somewhat differently:

The Law	The Prophets	The Writings
Genesis	Isaiah	Psalms
Exodus	Jeremiah	Proverbs
Leviticus	Ezekiel	Job
Numbers	Hosea	Esther
Deuteronomy	Joel	Song of Solomon
	Amos	Ruth
	Obadiah	Lamentations
	Jonah	Ecclesiastes
	Micah	Daniel
	Nahum	Ezra
	Habakkuk	Nehemiah
	Zephaniah	I Chronicles
	Haggai	II Chronicles
	Zechariah	
	Malachi	
	Joshua	
	Judges	
	I Samuel	
	II Samuel	
	I Kings	
	II Kings	

You will notice that the Law comprises the first five books of the Bible. These are also called the Pentateuch, a Greek word which means simply "five books." Written on scrolls, they were the first to be regarded as sacred by the Hebrews, long before there was any thought of combining them with other writings into a holy book. A copy of them is today kept in a place of honor in every Jewish synagogue.

These five books are likewise called "The Books of Moses."

This does not mean that Moses wrote them (although tradition assigns him as author) but that he is their central character. At the start of Exodus, the second book of the five, Moses enters the Bible story. It is the tale of how he was saved from Pharaoh's edict that all boy babies among the Hebrews be cast into the Nile. Moses was saved by being put in a basket of bulrushes which was daubed with bitumen and pitch and placed among the reeds at the river's brink. The last book of the five, Deuteronomy, closes with an account of the death of Moses. These five books include the Ten Commandments delivered to Moses and all the laws that were developed from them.

The Prophets, above, is headed by the three "major" prophets, Isaiah, Jeremiah, Ezekiel, followed by twelve "minor" prophets. However, by subject matter we would classify the book of Jonah as a biographical sketch since it is not the words of a prophet but a story concerning a prophet. The remaining six books: Joshua, Judges, I and II Samuel, I and II Kings, we would classify by subject matter as books of history.

This division into Law and Prophets is often referred to in later Hebrew writing. Jesus in the Sermon on the Mount, says, "Think not that I am come to destroy the law, or the prophets"; and elsewhere, "Thou shalt love the Lord thy God with all thy heart and with all thy soul and with all thy mind . . . and . . . thou shalt love thy neighbour as thyself. On these two commandments hang all the law and the prophets."

We will discuss the authorship of the Law and the Prophets in some detail on the following pages. The third group, known as the Writings, which is a miscellaneous collection of literature dealing with religious matters, will be discussed in Part IV.

When were the first five books, known as the Law, written? Read the first two chapters of Genesis very carefully and you may notice an unusual fact. There is not just one story of the Creation; there are two, each differing a bit in important details. Farther on, you will find that the story of Noah and the Flood is told in sentences that curiously overlap one another in information conveyed. Here are the two versions with the second italicized.

The Lord saw that the wickedness of man was great in the earth, and that every imagination of the thoughts of his heart was only evil continually. And the Lord was sorry that he had made man on the earth, and it grieved him to his heart. So the Lord said, "I will blot out man whom I have created from the face of the ground, man and beast and creeping things and birds of the air, for I am sorry that I have made them." But Noah found favor in the eyes of the Lord.

These are the generations of Noah. Noah was a righteous man, blameless in his generation; Noah walked with God. And Noah had three sons, Shem, Ham and Japheth.

Now the earth was corrupt in God's sight, and the earth was filled with violence. And God saw the earth, and behold, it was corrupt; for all flesh had corrupted their way upon the earth. And God said to Noah, "I have determined to make an end of all flesh; for the earth is filled with violence through them; behold, I will destroy them with the earth. Make yourself an ark of gopher wood; make rooms in the ark, and cover it inside and out with pitch."

Farther on, we find the story told doubly in this way:

Noah was six hundred years old when the flood of waters came upon the earth. And Noah and his sons and his wife and his sons' wives with him went into the ark, to escape the waters of the flood. Of clean animals, and of animals that are not clean, and of birds, and of everything that creeps on the ground, two and two, male and female, went into the ark with Noah, as God had commanded Noah. And after seven days the waters of the flood came upon the earth.

In the six hundredth year of Noah's life, in the second month, on the seventeenth day of the month, on that day all the fountains of the great deep burst forth, and the windows of the heavens were opened. And rain fell upon the earth forty days and forty nights. *On the very same day Noah and his sons, Shem and Ham and Japheth, and Noah's wife and the three wives of his sons with them entered the ark, they and every beast according to its kind, and all the cattle according to their kinds, and every creeping thing that creeps on the earth, according to its kind, and every bird according to its kind, every bird of every sort. They went into the ark with Noah, two and two of all flesh in which there was the breath of life. And they that entered, male and female of all flesh, went in as God had commanded him;* and the Lord shut him in.

Evidence like this occurs all through the first five books of the Bible, evidence that several strands were woven together (not always neatly) to form the books. Bible scholars have identified four chief strands and tagged them, for the sake of convenience, J, E, D and P, which stand for Judean, Ephraimite, Deuteronomic and Priestly. The passages quoted above are from J and P respectively.

To analyze the different parts of the Bible and explain why scholars believe one was written by J, another by E, and so forth, would be of no great value to the general reader. The important thing is to remember that these strands were finally woven together some time after the exile in Babylon, at a time when the Hebrews began to think about giving their library of religious writings more attention. Old scrolls were combined into new ones, the new ones were changed, cut and combined with still other scrolls. In this way the books as we know them finally took shape, although still written as scrolls.

Different biblical writers held different points of view. The Pentateuch covers so many subjects—early legends, history, ritual, law, action and ethics—partly because so many writers had a hand in its composition.

Of all the Old Testament books, the writings of the prophets are most likely to be the work of those whose names go with them. The outstanding exception to this is the book of Isaiah. The first thirty-nine chapters, much of which is narrative, partly borrowed from Kings, describe the life and give the words of a great statesman-prophet of the eighth century, B.C. But beginning with the fortieth chapter, the scene suddenly shifts. The sermons of the reformer of the southern kingdom give way to the glorious rhapsodies of a man who lived during the captivity, containing references to Babylon and to the Persian emperor Cyrus. This is discussed in greater detail in Part IV of this book.

As for the authorship of the book of Jeremiah, the answer seems to be found in its thirty-sixth chapter. On a cold December day in the year 604 B.C., King Jehoiakim sat in his winter palace keeping warm by the fire. Someone brought him a set of scrolls containing a series of sermons that a man named Baruch had read aloud to the people gathered by the Temple gate. They were actually the words of that archdisturber, Jeremiah, with whom the king had had trouble before and who was now living in hiding.

The king began to read the scrolls. As usual they were bold tirades against the government and the king's policies because they did not follow the word of God. As the king finished each scroll he slit it with his penknife and threw it in the fire.

When Jeremiah heard this, the record tells us, he took fresh scrolls and with Baruch still serving as his secretary dictated a whole new volume of prophecy. It contained all the material in the old scrolls and much more besides. This second set of scrolls was more carefully guarded than the first and the probability is that we have them today as the major part of the book of Jeremiah.

We can be reasonably certain that the other books bearing the names of prophets were their own work, preserved either by transcription as the words were delivered, or later dictation by the speaker himself.

The six books of history, Joshua, Judges, I and II Samuel and I and II Kings, are anonymous too. Bits and pieces of them were written by writers ranging over four or five centuries, beginning with the twelfth century B.C., and then all were welded into the books as we know them by an editor living probably between 600 and 500 B.C. By this process old texts were embedded in later writings like precious stones in a new setting. For example, the Ode of Deborah found in the fifth chapter of Judges has the earmarks of having been written down on the very day of the victory it celebrates—over Sisera, the Canaanite leader, who must have lived in the twelfth century B.C.

Probably the earliest book of consecutive history-writing in the world is the story of David told in the books of Samuel. It must have been written by someone in David's court who knew him well. One theory is that the chapters were written by Abiathar. The reasoning goes this way: Abiathar became David's priest when David was an outlaw living in the cave of Adullam. At the time of David's death, years later, Abiathar supported the claim of Adonijah, David's fourth son, to the throne, rather than that of Solomon. But Solomon won

he throne and banished Abiathar. He felt the priest de-
erved execution as a traitor but because he was so old and
ad been loyal to Solomon's father, David, Solomon merely
anished him.

Being a priest, Abiathar could write, which few people
ould do in those days. How very likely, then, that in his re-
irement Abiathar sat down to write the earliest story of the
ounding of the Hebrew monarchy.

We think this account was an eyewitness report because
o many details of it are drawn from life. If it had been writ-
en later, many of the intimate touches would have been
mitted, and it would have given us merely the picture of an
deal king in a picturesque court. But the stories are too
onest and too vivid to be anything but the work of a man
vith firsthand familiarity with the events.

As noted earlier, besides the Law and the Prophets, the
Iebrew scriptures eventually included the books called the
Vritings. Since the authorship of each of these merits a
eparate discussion, we shall reserve it for Part IV of this
ook, when we shall go over the Writings in some detail.

What was the appearance of the scrolls on which were writ-
en the words later to become our Bible? We can learn how
hey looked because of some very recent discoveries. In the
pring of 1947, some Arab herdsmen were looking for a stray
goat along the shores of the Dead Sea. High up on one of
he cliffs, one of the herdsmen saw a cave. Thinking the
goat might have wandered in there, he climbed up and en-
ered. Inside he found a great number of jars. Some of the
ars contained ancient scrolls. One of the scrolls was a beau-
ifully penned manuscript of the words of the prophet Isaiah,
about twenty-four feet long and about twelve inches high.
It had been written in ink on seventeen sheets of coarse
parchment (scraped and dried animal skins), sewn together

with linen thread. The text was in Hebrew and showed signs of having been used a great deal. Experts believe that this Isaiah scroll dates from about the year 100 B.C., or a bit earlier.

Tracing the authorship of the New Testament books is less complicated; it calls for less detective work. In the New Testament many of the writers can be verified.

We will start not with the usual order of the New Testament books, as they appear in traditional editions of the Bible, but with the event which sparked the spiritual revolution which has since swept the world: the death and resurrection of Jesus. From that central event we can uncover the order in which the books appeared, and to some extent, how near or far in time they fell from that event. Of course, in these matters there is still divergence of opinion among scholars.

Apparently, the letters of Paul, of all the writings in the New Testament, were closest in time of composition to the life of Christ. Paul was converted to Christianity only a few months after the death of Jesus, and in a few years went on the first of his missionary journeys. On his second journey around the year A.D. 50, just twenty short years after the crucifixion, he wrote the earliest of his letters we have today. This is his first letter to the Thessalonians. Between the year 50 and Paul's death, probably fourteen years later, he wrote all the letters we now have.

Although Paul's letters tell us a great deal about his work and the churches he established, they tell almost nothing about the life and actual words of Jesus. One reason for this may have been the fact that the memory of Jesus was still fresh; his life and messages did not seem to need retelling. People still lived who had watched him hold the crowds spellbound with his parables; children, now grown, remem-

ered how he had laid hands on them to bless them; there
were women in Galilee and Jerusalem who recalled having
prepared food for him. And beyond these were the countless
multitudes who had heard about him from people who had
come under his spell. Perhaps Paul did not give us more of
his master's earthly life because he was surrounded by people
with firsthand memories of it whereas he himself had probably never met Jesus.

But in time all this changed.

The apostles died, one by one. The men and women with
personal recollections were gone or going. Memories of Jesus
were in danger of becoming family hand-me-downs, subject
to lapses, exaggerations and distortions. The need for a voice
to speak with authority about his life and teachings became
clear.

But it was too late to find a man who could write what he
himself had heard Jesus say. The best that could be found
were men who could write down what the *disciples* had said
about Jesus, and what they might pick up from the incomplete and contradictory written reports then in circulation.

Mark was the first of these men whose gospels or "good
news" have come down to us. Mark—John Mark to give him
his full name—was the close companion of great Christian
leaders for thirty-five years, helping them carry the gospel to
the outside world. He had been a companion of both Paul
and Peter. He watched them at work and heard them speak
on all sorts of occasions.

Mark may very well have been Peter's interpreter in the
places which they visited. Greek was the tongue of most
cities and of the educated classes, and we can be sure that
Peter's Greek was not of the best, if he spoke it at all; as a
fisherman on the Sea of Galilee he would not have had much
chance to learn it in his youth. Through his work as inter-

preter, Mark must have had an intimate glimpse of Peter'
memories of Jesus. And more than that, Peter's way of put
ting things, his favorite expressions and unique ways of tell
ing of Christ, must have stuck in Mark's memory because o
his daily work of interpreting. What could better assure u
that Mark's gospel is an accurate reflection of Peter'
thoughts? No one was personally better fitted than Mark t
preserve in writing all that Peter taught and felt about Jesus

What was the immediate reason for Mark to take the tim
and trouble to record the literal words of Peter about Jesus

Early tradition has it that both Peter and Paul died in th
year A.D. 64, during Nero's persecution of the Christians ir
Rome. It is not hard to imagine how the little band o
Christ-followers in Rome felt after their great leaders ha
been executed: unsure of themselves; stripped of their per
sonal link to Jesus; remote from his birthplace, which mos
of them had doubtless never visited; and always waiting fo
the loud knock in the night which might signify arrest and
martyrdom.

It was in this crisis that Mark gave us his gift. He decide
to write an account of Jesus' life and ministry to take th
place of Peter's now silent voice. He probably wrote be
tween A.D. 65 and 70.

Our most reliable authority for Mark's authorship is Pa
pias, a bishop in the early church about the year A.D. 140
Papias was told about Mark by a certain church elder—whicl
takes us back fairly close to the date of Mark himself. Her
is what the elder told Papias:

> Mark, having become Peter's interpreter, wrote down ac-
> curately, though not in order, as many as he remembered
> of the things said or done by the Lord. For he neither had
> heard the Lord nor followed him, but at a later time he
> followed Peter . . . So that Mark made no mistake, thus

writing down some things as he remembered them; for of one thing he took forethought, namely not to leave out any one of the things he had heard or to state falsely anything in them.

The early Christians must have felt greatly comforted by he record of Jesus now set down in black and white. They ncorporated readings from it into their worship services, vhere they have remained to this day.

A principal reason for assigning to Mark an earlier date han Matthew is that we will discover, if we care to do so, hat of Mark's six hundred and sixty-one verses, Matthew eproduces six hundred almost word for word. When Matthew sat down to write his gospel he surely had a copy of Mark before him.

But why did Matthew sit down to write another gospel at ll? Apparently because he wanted to present Jesus not only s a man of action but as a great teacher. Where Mark was pparently writing for Romans, Matthew was writing for ews. He refers continually to the fulfillment of the prophe-ies of the Old Testament.

Matthew had access to much material that Mark did not, specially the teachings of Jesus. Into Mark's outline he in-erts these teachings, for the most part in five great blocks. The first and most famous is in Chapters 5, 6 and 7, the Ser-mon on the Mount. In Chapter 10 we have the second, con-isting of special directions for the disciples. In the thirteenth hapter we find a group of parables about the coming of the ingdom of heaven on earth. The other sayings are in the ighteenth and in the twenty-fourth and twenty-fifth chap-ers. None of this material is in Mark.

The date of Matthew's gospel has long been a matter of arnest research as to whether it came before the fall of Jeru-alem under Titus in A.D. 70 or afterward. To the ordinary

reader this is of little concern. We are grateful to this later
writer for two things: first, for sensing the authority of Mark's
record—proved by his using it—and second, for preserving
the priceless words of Jesus. In the Sermon on the Moun
alone we have the Beatitudes, the Lord's Prayer and the
Golden Rule.

The writings of Luke in the New Testament are in two
parts: his gospel and his sequel to it, The Acts of the Apos
tles. The first is a biography of Christ similar to the earlier
gospels; the second carries the story beyond the crucifixion
to the early days of the founding of the Christian Church

Many readers approaching the Bible for the first time be
lieve that the four gospels are so much alike that it was un
necessary to have included them all. They content them
selves with picking one to read, then skip the others. This i
a mistake. Although there are many points of similarity
among them, they are also very different, as we have already
seen in comparing Matthew and Mark. Each illuminates a
separate aspect of the life and teachings of Jesus. They add
up together to a more complete portrait of him than any one
alone could do. For the fullest picture of Jesus, it is neces
sary to read all the gospels.

We have seen that Mark's gospel was mainly a historical
record, full of eyewitness detail, sincere but unpolished. Mat
thew's gospel added to Mark's a collection of memorable
teachings. But the two volumes of Luke were written to fil
another need. Luke was a Gentile. The Christian movement
was bursting the bounds of Judaism and was attracting Gen
tiles both of the humbler sort and educated people. Luke
was writing particularly for the latter.

Luke writes with a practiced hand. He was a man of let
ters, quoting in his first two chapters some of the poetry of
the day that has since immeasurably enriched our Christmas

observances. His gospel has been called the most beautiful
book ever written. He seeks to offend nothing the Romans
held dear while at the same time he presents Jesus, not merely
as a miracle-worker as Mark had done or as the promised
Jewish Messiah as Matthew had done, but as the Savior of
the world, the founder of a new religion.

Luke's two-part volume was probably written between 85
and A.D. 95, possibly at the same time as Matthew's.
Together with his Acts, it was immensely popular among
the early Christians. As it began to find its way among the
churches of Greece and Asia Minor, the people who had
known Paul and had copies of his letters in their church
chests, became aware of what a great man Paul had become.
They got out their letters and were soon besieged with re-
quests for copies of them. And so it came about that Paul's
letters (and with them letters attributed to disciples Peter,
James and John and to Jude) took so prominent a place
among early church documents that they were eventually
included in the official scriptures.

Before John wrote his gospel (the fourth and last of the
gospels), apparently much later than the others, a great deal
had happened. Among other things fantastic ideas about the
unreality of Jesus' earthly life were being taught. John's gospel is aimed in part at thwarting these ideas. It is a message
that seeks to establish Christ as completely human and completely divine. It does not contain the Sermon on the Mount,
nor any of the parables. It mentions the Kingdom of God
but twice. But in John's gospel the reader finds the living
Christ talking to him, directly. That is why it is to many
people the most precious of the gospels, if not the most beloved of all the books of the Bible. Its purpose is clearly
stated in one of its closing sentences, "These are written

that you may believe that Jesus is the Christ . . . and that believing you may have life in his name."

After reading the gospel of John it is a good idea to read the three letters and the book of Revelation, which also bear his name.

The early church realized that each gospel made its own contribution to the understanding of Jesus, and consistently preserved these four gospels among the many other writings about Jesus. Matthew, Mark, Luke and John carried the authority that goes with the writings of those who had the privilege of hearing from eyewitnesses the actual facts of Christ's deeds and words.

The letter to the Hebrews is considered by many scholars the most literary of all New Testament books and is anonymous. Actually it is more like a sermon than a letter, full of ornate phrases. Some experts believe it was written by a church leader of Rome, who wrote it to his congregation at Rome while he was away travelling.

So far we have discussed only individual books of the Bible and, indeed, only a few of those. We have seen how many of the Old Testament books were created in various ways: by the work, first, of original writers, then editors who brought the earlier writings together into larger books; through the foresight of prophets who wrote or dictated their words. We have seen how the New Testament books grew from the great need for a written record of the life of Jesus, and from the gradual realization that Paul's letters (and those of some other apostles) had great religious and historical value.

But we have not yet discussed the Bible as a single volume. We must be aware that the Bible as one book, or even the thought of it, did not exist from the very beginning. For

centuries the sacred words were contained only in a collection of separate scrolls, individually stored and read. It was
not until comparatively late, in A.D. 90, that the Jewish authorities finally decided on all the writings which ought to
be united in an official scripture, or canon, of Jewish religious literature. However, a certain formalization had taken
place before this in the case of the Law and the Prophets.
These scrolls had a special and sacred authority of their own,
due to their age and contents; the decision in A.D. 90 chiefly
concerned other scrolls which would accompany the Law
and Prophets in the canon, and which were to be known as
the Writings.

Likewise, it was not until a great Christian council was
held in Carthage in A.D. 397, that the church fathers decided
which documents ought to be officially adopted by the church
and which ought to be left out. Our Bible, as a Bible, dates
from these two events.

This means that in the time of Jesus and in the years just
after, there was no Old Testament as we know it. True, there
were the ancient writings of the Hebrews and Jesus refers to
these as "the law and the prophets," but these were still available only on separate scrolls and were not thought of as one
book or Testament. In the fourth chapter of Luke the story
is told how Jesus, when he visited his home town of Nazareth
and was invited to speak in the synagogue, read from the
scroll of Isaiah, from what we call today the sixty-first chapter. The scroll he used may well have been much like the
scroll of Isaiah found in 1947 above the Dead Sea.

How was the decision made for both the Old and New
Testaments to include some writings and omit others?

In the case of the Old Testament its final form might be
said to have come about as the result of a political crisis. In
A.D. 67, the Hebrews revolted against Rome, a suicidal at-

tempt to break the grip of the strongest nation on earth. The results were disastrous. After dreadful fighting and massacre, the holy city of Jerusalem was retaken by the Romans under Titus in A.D. 70. It was sacked and burned to the ground. The Temple that had been built by Herod the Great was destroyed. Its golden vessels and sacred scrolls were loaded aboard Roman galleys for display in the victory parade in Rome.

A teacher of Jerusalem, however, one Johanan ben Zakkai, had managed to salvage copies of the sacred scrolls before the city was destroyed. These he took to the small town of Jamnia, thirty miles outside Jerusalem. There he started a school, to keep the tradition of the priesthood alive; and there in A.D. 90, twenty years after the last destruction of the nation, noted Jewish scholars met to decide which books—in addition to the already accepted Law and Prophets—should be classified as sacred. Reading and rereading the scrolls, the learned men argued the merits of each. Their discussions at this time finally settled the question of which additional scrolls should be canonized. These became known as the Writings.

Many books were omitted, books which had perhaps been popular in certain areas and with certain groups. Some of these omitted books have come to be known as the apocryphal (meaning hidden or secret) books of the Bible. They are also referred to as the Apocrypha. In this country, the apocryphal books are part of the official Bible of the Episcopal and Roman Catholic churches. They are not included in the official Bible of other Protestant churches nor of the Jews. The reason why they are found in some Bibles and not in others is due to a complicated sequence of events, which we will touch on briefly.

The Jews who had left their homeland, beginning with

the upheaval of the Babylonian invasions and continuing through the difficult centuries afterwards, scattered far and wide over the Mediterranean area. Many went to Egypt, where their numbers increased until about one of every eight persons was a Jew. With the spread of Greek culture in the wake of Alexander's conquests and the founding of his name-sake-city of Alexandria, many Jews learned Greek and forgot their ancient tongue. Alexandria was a Greek-speaking city and when the Law and the Prophets were read there in the synagogue, they had to be followed by a translation or ex-planation in Greek. A Greek translation of the Bible became necessary. The translation, when it was made, possibly around the year 250 B.C., was called the Septuagint, a Latin word meaning seventy—for the seventy scholars traditionally said to have done the work.

But at the time of the translation only the Law and the Prophets had been officially recognized and canonized by the Jewish authorities. The other group, the Writings, was still an undefined group of scrolls with wide popular circulation. The Septuagint translators included many works of this fluid collection in their new translation. In this way the books we know today as the Apocrypha probably found their way into the Septuagint.

When the time came for Jerome to make his monumental translation of the scriptures into Latin about six hundred and fifty years later, in A.D. 400, the Writings *had* been fixed upon and the Jewish canon included some and not others. But Jerome came across some in the Septuagint that were not included in the Jewish canon, due to the fact that the Septuagint translation had been made before the Writings were officially examined and a selection of them made.

Apparently Jerome was at first in a quandary as to whether to include these "semi-official" Writings in his new definitive translation. First he omitted them altogether. Then he translated some as "good for edification" but "not for proving the doctrines of the church." By finally being incorporated in Jerome's translation, the Apocrypha became and still are part of the official Bible of the Roman Catholic Church, since the Catholic Church adopted Jerome's translation as its official text. They were scattered throughout the text of the Catholic Bible as seemed most appropriate.

When Luther in the sixteenth century made his German translation he included these books but, because they were not a part of the Hebrew canon, assembled them together between the Testaments. The Church of England followed Luther's arrangement. But the Puritans rejected them with the result that today in this country, while they are used by the Episcopal and Catholic churches, they are seldom found in other Bibles.

The contents of the Apocrypha differ from one list to another, but the books traditionally contained in the English versions number fourteen:

> I and II Esdras
> Tobit
> Judith
> Rest of the Book of Esther
> Wisdom of Solomon
> Ecclesiasticus
> I and II Maccabees
> Baruch, including the Epistle of Jeremy
> Additions to the Book of Daniel:
>> Song of the Three Children
>> Susanna
>> Bel and the Dragon
> Prayer of Manasses

This miscellaneous collection of all kinds and styles of writing is typical of the many-sided Jewish genius. Tobit,

Judith and Susanna may be classified as biographical sketches, or stories about individuals. I Esdras is a retelling of history; II Esdras belongs in the category of "apocalyptic literature," which will be explained later. The books of the Maccabees are straightforward historical narrative. Ecclesiasticus and the Wisdom of Solomon are philosophical works; Baruch is prophecy; Bel and the Dragon is myth.

To return, however, to the earlier Christian church, it regarded the Hebrew writings as its sacred writings and for most of the first century its only ones. Peter used quotations from them to prove his points, and when Paul said he "reasoned with them out of the scriptures" the only scriptures he meant were the ancient Hebrew ones. But gradually, as we have seen, Christianity felt the need of producing its own writings, not to replace the ancient ones but to supplement them. We can imagine a flood of writings pouring from the enthusiastic hearts of early Christians, which created the problem of choosing from them those meriting official sanction.

The answer was found in two centuries of use. Out of the wealth of writings, certain books came to be used and treasured and believed more than others. They emerged as the books with the power to sway men's minds for the new religion. In reality, the New Testament was selected by the thousands of Christians who listened to readings from many books Sunday after Sunday and placed their faith in some writings rather than in others. When the great church council was held in Carthage in A.D. 397 to settle for all time which books should be bound into one New Testament, it had the reactions of two centuries of Christian use to guide it. Certain books *had* to be included; others had not earned that right.

It was probably about this same time that the Old and

New Testaments began to be bound together in one volume. Some time before this, leaf books—more or less like our own today—had taken the place of the clumsy scrolls which had to be unrolled and could not contain too many words because the longer they were the more inconvenient to handle.

As the two groups of writings began to be bound together, it became necessary to distinguish between the parts. Now the Hebrews had regarded their religion as a covenant with God, first made by Abraham. The Christians, possibly recalling from the book of Jeremiah the prophet's vision which had also been quoted in their own book of Hebrews, hit upon the designation "The Old and the New Covenants (or Testaments)" as the best names for the two parts. Here is what Jeremiah had said:

> Behold, the days come, saith the Lord, that I will make a new covenant with the house of Israel, and with the house of Judah: not according to the covenant that I made with their fathers in the day that I took them by the hand to bring them out of the land of Egypt; which my covenant they broke, although I was an husband unto them, saith the Lord: but this shall be the covenant that I will make with the house of Israel: After those days, saith the Lord, I will put my law in their inward parts, and write it in their hearts; and will be their God, and they shall be my people.

And thus the newly bound Bible, with two great bodies of religious writing, came to be called the Old Testament and the New Testament. And so they have been called to this day.

It is interesting to note that the English word "Bible" as applied to a volume containing the Old and the New Testaments stems from fairly modern times. It was not even in common use at the time of the appearance of the King James version in 1611. In all the thousands of pages of Shakespeare's works the word "Bible" does not occur once, although holy writ, scripture, scriptures and gospel often do.

Since the scriptures adopted by the Christian church were in Greek, translations came to be needed as the missionaries of Christ pushed their way out into the Roman empire. Among the first to be made were those for the Christians in Egypt, who spoke the Coptic and Ethiopic languages, and that great group to the north of the Holy Land which spoke Syriac. The Syriac translation went with the missionaries as far west as present-day Germany and as far east as Ceylon, India and China.

Meanwhile, Latin had become the official language of the vast Roman Empire, and parts of the scriptures had often been translated into this tongue. However, many of these earlier translations were incomplete and full of errors. Therefore, in A.D. 382 Damasus, Bishop of Rome, appointed the greatest scholar of his day, Eusebius Sophronius Hieronymus, whom we know as Jerome, to make a dependable translation of the entire Bible into Latin, both Old and New Testaments. To do his work thoroughly, Jerome lived in the Holy Land for twenty years, where he immersed himself in Jewish life, studied with the leading rabbis, and examined every manuscript he could find.

His translation into the common language of the people called *vulgus*, came to be known as the Latin Vulgate. Though it was not immediately accepted (no new version of the Bible ever is) it eventually (on April 8, 1546) became the official text of the Roman Catholic Church and has remained so.

The Latin Vulgate is one of the truly great Bibles of Christian history. It was the principal version that accompanied the Christians as they penetrated Europe, winning converts as they went. All through the Dark Ages this was the Bible which more than any other kept the candle of faith burning, as devout monks made faithful copies and from it translated the Bible into other tongues.

Chapter 12

How the Bible Came To Us in English

THE FIRST complete Bible in English was translated from the Latin Vulgate, under the inspiring leadership of John Wycliffe, who lived in England one hundred years before Columbus discovered America. It was also one hundred years before any other nation in Europe had the Bible in its own tongue.

John Wycliffe was what we might call a "go-getter." He bristled with ideas, a rare combination of the scholar and the man of initiative. Determined to do something for the religious life of England, he gathered around him other scholars who translated the whole Latin Bible into English. Printing had not yet been invented, and every copy of his Bible had to be written out by hand. But hundreds of them must have been made, for there are more than one hundred and seventy copies surviving to this day.

Wycliffe's Bible was a translation from a translation, and not a very careful one at that. But the actual English wording of Wycliffe's Bible was of the best, for he was a master of the English of his day.

The manuscript copies of Wycliffe's Bible, while very expensive, became immensely popular. Though persistent persecution dogged the steps of those possessing the book, it was

171

widely read during the fifteenth century. It is related that as much as five marks (the equivalent of two hundred dollars today) was paid for one copy and that a farmer gave a load of hay for a chapter or two of the book of James.

The average English reader of today would have a hard time with the text of Wycliffe's Bible. Written in the language used by Chaucer, it is as difficult for us to read as are Chaucer's *Canterbury Tales* in their original form.

It is William Tyndale, born about a hundred years after Wycliffe, who is the father of the English Bible as we know it. Tyndale was a pre-eminent scholar. After ten years at Oxford and Cambridge, says one of his biographers, he became so skilled in the seven languages—Hebrew, Greek, Latin, Italian, Spanish, English and French—that one would suppose each of them was his native tongue. He was also a reformer with a passion. Distressed by the ignorance, conservatism, and indifference of many of the clergy of his day, he was determined that the people should hear the word of God for themselves.

To one of the leaders of the church he said, "If God spare my life, ere many years I will cause a boy that driveth a plow to know more of the scriptures than thou dost." For, as he said later, "I had perceaved by experyence, how that it was impossible to stablysh the laye people in any truth, excepte the scripture were playnly layde before their eyes in their mother tonge, that they might se the processe, ordre and meanings of the texte . . ."

Tyndale had something of the practical promoter in him too. When he translated the scriptures into English, he would not merely produce manuscripts. He would see the work through the press, so that the books might be broadcast by the thousands, since printing by movable metallic type had been invented by Gutenberg in Germany in 1456.

But beyond all these qualifications, Tyndale had two that were supreme. He achieved unerring mastery of the English language at the very moment it was budding into flower, so that his version fixed our standard English once for all. And finally, he was made of the stuff of martyrs. At all costs he would see his program through. And he paid the final price. For, finding that he would not be tolerated in England if he put the scriptures into the native tongue there, he left his native land, never to return. In 1524, when he was forty years old, he became convinced that there was no place in England where he would be unmolested in his work. Germany and Holland were, in those days, the liberal countries of Europe. Tyndale began his work of printing the New Testament in Cologne in 1525.

But enemies were dogging his steps, and Tyndale had to move around the continent to avoid them. Meanwhile his New Testaments were finding their way back to England, smuggled in under false covers. In the diary of a German scholar of those days we read that the English people, in spite of the opposition of their king, were so eager for the gospel that some declared they would buy a New Testament even if they had to pay a hundred thousand pieces of money for it.

Finally after twelve exciting years on the continent, with the task uncompleted, being betrayed by one supposed to be a friend, William Tyndale was thrown into prison, strangled and his body burned.

Tyndale's dying prayer is a classic of English history: "Lord, open the King of England's eyes." The prayer was swiftly answered; for even while Tyndale was languishing in prison Miles Coverdale's translation, incorporating almost all of Tyndale's work, did become by royal consent the open book of the English people. Its reception was instant, widespread and enthusiastic. Through the next seventy-five years, translation after translation appeared, but they were all based on Tyndale's pioneer work. Of the King James Bible, about eighty per cent of the Old Testament and ninety per cent of the New are Tyndale's.

The English version for the use of Roman Catholic readers has a different history, however. During the early part of the reign of Queen Elizabeth of England, certain prominent Catholics had left England in fear of persecution. These exiles found refuge first in the French city of Rheims and later in Douai. They established a college at Douai and the scholars among them translated the scriptures, the New Testament translation being finished in 1582 in Rheims, the Old Testament in 1609 in Douai.

The Rheims-Douai Bible was translated directly from the Vulgate of Jerome and many of his old Latin words reappear in it. Catholic scholars in recent years have been bringing out a radical revision of the Rheims-Douai Bible into modern English which, though it is called a translation from the Latin Vulgate, is based on exhaustive present-day studies of the original Hebrew and Greek.

And now we come to the most famous Bible translation of all, and probably the most famous translation of any book in the world's history. It is the King James, or Authorized Version, of the Bible published in England in 1611.

When James I came to the throne in 1603, England had become a first-class nation. The Spanish Armada had been defeated; the East India Company had been formed; the colonizing of America was in the offing. English literature was bursting into full flower with Shakespeare, Marlowe, Bacon, Spenser and others. But things religious in England were in a bad way when James came to the throne. The Established Church and the Puritans were at loggerheads. James called a conference to straighten out these matters.

Although there were various English Bibles in use, some preferred by the Established Church and others by the Puritans, apparently the authorization of a single version of the Bible was not on the docket of this conference. It came up, however, almost by accident, on the last day of the meeting and King James took action. It was the best thing he ever did, and he did it well.

Fifty-four men were selected to do the work, which lasted for at least four years. Our King James Version appeared in 1611. So acceptable was it that, although there had been six or seven major revisions of the Bible in the seventy-five years between Tyndale's New Testament and the appearance of the King James, this new version gradually forged to the front and no one proposed a major revision of it for at least two hundred and seventy years.

With the consecrated genius of Tyndale as its foundation, the King James Bible—the work of the best scholars of the day, produced at the very moment when the genius of the language for noble prose was at its height—became what Professor William Lyon Phelps of Yale has called "the most beautiful book in the world in any language, a book which has exercised an incalculable influence upon religion, upon manners, upon literature and upon character."

The Bible in English illustrates the living power of the scriptures. Though all agree that the King James Version is a masterpiece of English literature, it has not been allowed to entomb the Bible itself. Lately many translations have been made anew in English as manuscripts with better texts are discovered, problems in the ancient languages of the Bible are solved, and as the English tongue grows and changes.

Every scholarly new translation of the English Bible is a forward step to the understanding of the scriptures. It stimulates readers to reach again to the heart of the Bible's message, rather than skim over some of the familiar phrases of the King James version. It cuts a new groove in men's thinking. Granted that the King James will probably never be matched for majesty and power of utterance yet each good new translation makes its own contribution to our enjoyment and understanding of the Bible.

Through the persistent and sacrificial ministry of Christian missionaries the Bible has become, as no other book, "the World's Book." By 1956, some part of the Bible had been translated and published in 1092 languages, of which 207 now have the whole Bible, 265 others have the whole New Testament, and 620 others have at least a whole book of the Bible. There is more biblical translation and revision work going on just now than ever in Christian history.

Interestingly, almost everyone thinks the Bible in *his* language is the original Bible. A Chinese father in Manchuria some years ago wrote to the Bible Society office in Mukden as follows: "My son is going off to the big city to college. There he will be studying in English. Would you tell me, sir, has the Bible yet been translated into English? If so, I would like to have a copy for my son."

The list of languages possessing some part of the Bible is growing at the rate of about one new language every month, a rate that has been maintained for over fifty years. In this respect, the Bible may well be called the miracle of world literature.

PART FOUR

Traveling Through the Bible

Chapter 13

The Mighty Deeds of the Lord

MANY READERS feel honor-bound to "finish" the Bible once they have started it. They think a book not properly read until every word has been absorbed. This idea, a commendable one when applied to many books, does not fit the Bible at all; it may only produce unhappy results. It must be admitted that some parts of the Bible are better than others for the general reader.

The purpose of this section is to direct your attention to the more rewarding sections of the Bible, and to issue warnings about other parts. There is no reason to feel that you do the book an injustice by leaving certain parts to scholars, historians and antiquarians. By so doing you only keep yourself free to absorb its great messages, your mind uncluttered by data like genealogies, legal codes and building specifications.

Every page of the Bible is a treasure house for the student of ancient faiths, Jewish law and the history of religious thought. But the reader who wants the world of today explained, as only the Bible can explain it, will profit more by reading and rereading certain sections and skipping others.

As an example of the kind of passage that might first bore, then discourage you with the whole Bible, take the seventh chapter of the book of Numbers. It is an elaborate description of the offerings brought for the dedication of the tabernacle built by Moses. Each of the twelve tribes is given his due in the text, which is a minute list of the offerings brought:

> On the second day, Nethanel the son of Zuar, the leader of Issachar, made an offering; he offered for his offering one silver plate, whose weight was a hundred and thirty shekels, one silver basin of seventy shekels, according to the shekel of the sanctuary, both of them full of fine flour mixed with oil for a cereal offering; one golden dish of ten shekels, full of incense. . . .

And so on for eighty-nine verses.

The Bible has reading in it that deserves and earns your attention. Passages like the one above are few but it is important to avoid them in your first encounter with the book.

The first sixteen books of the Old Testament may be roughly classified as books of history. The best way to read them is in sizable chunks, preferably a book at a time. When you settle down to read them, set aside an evening or a Sunday afternoon. By so doing you can feel the sweep of time covered by each narrative.

The historical books of the Bible give a consecutive narrative of events from the creation to the days reported by Ezra and Nehemiah following the exile in Babylon. Here, then, are the books, with suggestions on what to read.

Genesis. Genesis is rewarding reading in its entirety. It falls naturally into five sections:

1. Adam and Eve, The First Man and Woman. Chapters 1 to 5.

2. Noah and the Great Flood. Chapters 6 to 11. (The genealogies in this section may be omitted).

3. The Covenant of God with Abraham. Chapters 11 to 25.

4. Jacob, Founder of the Nation. Chapters 26 to 35.

5. Joseph and his Brothers. Chapters 37 to 50.

Exodus. Moses is the hero of Exodus and the flight from Egypt is described in the first twenty chapters. This stirring story should be read at one sitting, if possible; notice that the Ten Commandments occur in Chapter 20. Chapters 21 to 24 ascribe to Moses some of the oldest civil and religious laws, including the Book of the Covenant, to be found in the Old Testament. They are well worth your attention. However, the next six chapters, 25 to 31, can be omitted. They give the detailed plans for building the tabernacle. The rest of the book, except the impressive last chapter, 40, need not be read.

Leviticus. This book can be omitted too, unless you are interested in a detailed study of the Jewish law. It is really a book of instructions for the priests of the Temple.

Numbers. This book is good reading from Chapter 10 through Chapter 14, and from Chapter 20 through Chapter 24. Its Hebrew title, "In The Wilderness," is more appropriate than the one we know, for the term "Numbers" is descriptive only of Chapters 1 to 4 and 26, which tell of the official census taken of the twelve tribes. In the chapters recommended, this book has the same drive and vigor found in Genesis and the early chapters of Exodus.

Deuteronomy. This is the book which many of today's best scholars believe was found in the Temple in the reign of Josiah, and which sparked a wave of reform in worship and of observance of the Jewish law. In literary quality it is among the very best of the Bible; it has been called the Gospel of the Old Testament. Its recurring theme is God's love for his people, eloquently combining the ideal of loyalty to the law of God with the truth of God's love for Israel. Ex-

cept for the opening and closing chapters it is not narrative
It is a rewriting of the earlier laws and so naturally is dedi
cated to Moses, concluding with a moving account of Moses
death and burial, as the grand old patriarch is taken to the
top of the mountain that overlooks the promised land, and
hears the Lord say, "This is the land of which I swore to
Abraham, to Isaac, and to Jacob, saying 'I will give it to
your descendants': I have let you see it with your eyes but
you shall not go over there." Chapters 12 to 26 which give
minor laws, need not be read. Chapters 32 and 33, however,
called respectively "The Song of Moses" and "The Blessing
of Moses," are definitely "musts."

Joshua. So closely does the story in this book follow that
in the first five books that it is sometimes linked up with
them. The first five are together called the Pentateuch
(meaning "five books"). When Joshua is included with them
the term Hexateuch ("six books") is used. Joshua is a thrilling story of the conquest of Canaan. It gives the impression
that the conquest was accomplished swiftly and completely,
but the first verse of the thirteenth chapter serves as the key
to the actual situation. Here the Lord says to Joshua, "You
are old and advanced in years, and there remains yet very
much land to be possessed." Archaeological research, which
has substantiated many of the events in the book, would indicate that the conquest took almost two centuries. Joshua
is absorbing reading, full of strategy and drama. For the beginner, few Old Testament books make better reading.

Judges. Like Genesis, the book of Judges presents great
hero-figures and you need no introduction to them but the
power of your reading imagination. Deborah, Gideon, Jeph-
thah and the tragic Samson walk the pages of this book, and
their stories are among the great ones of the Bible.

The phrase, "Every man did that which was right in his

own eyes," crops up quite often in this book, typical of the lawless spirit of new civilizations, before the beginnings of more stable national life; typical, too, of the early days of our own West.

The song of Deborah in Chapter 5 may well be the oldest piece of writing in the entire Bible; it was written in the turbulent years of the conquest of the promised land, between 1200 and 1000 B.C. It tells in trumpet-toned poetry of the triumph of the Israelites over the Canaanite army.

The editor of the book of Judges saved this saga, which had probably been circulating from campfire to campfire for hundreds of years, by writing it down and including it in his book. By so doing, he preserved for us an example of the beginning of a great national literature. It is a kind of fossil-remain of the folk tales which were passed from mouth to mouth for centuries, and which were finally immortalized in our Bible.

I and II Samuel. These two books, containing the unforgettable stories of Samuel the prophet, King Saul and his successor, King David, are the crown of historical writing in the Old Testament. They should be read entire; the two books taken together can be covered during a long afternoon. The stories come brilliantly alive; it is hard to find more exciting writing even in the most modern novel.

I and II Kings. These books cover most of the story of the united Hebrew kingdom and later of the separate northern and southern kingdoms until the fall of each. Thus it takes you up to the exile. The story of Solomon's fabulous reign occupies the first eleven chapters of I Kings. Skipping Chapters 6 and 7, which give detailed descriptions of Solomon's Temple, this section makes an absorbing sequel to the stories of David, Solomon's father. The last eleven chapters of the book present a less unified narrative, but abound in stories of stirring events, including especially the deeds of the prophet Elijah. The second book of Kings begins with the story of Elisha (the first eight chapters), and tells the sad story of the fall of the northern kingdom and, later, the captivity and destruction of Jerusalem.

Chapters 18-20 of II Kings are almost identical with Chapters 36-39 of Isaiah. The first thirty-nine chapters of Isaiah reflect the days of the long decline of Judah and go well with your reading of II Kings.

I and II Chronicles. These two books cover the same period as II Samuel and the two books of Kings, but were written much later. They can both be skipped since they add little new material and are written in a repetitious, formal style. If you want to return to them later, after having become acquainted with the great moments of the Old Testament, you may find they cast light on some hitherto obscure incidents of Hebrew history. But when you are first reading the Old Testament to introduce yourself to its best parts, these books are better omitted.

Ezra and Nehemiah. These two books should be read together. Indeed, in the Hebrew Bible they are combined as one book. As history they are not as full and rich as some of the earlier books, but they are our only (though fragmentary) record of the days when the exile had ended and the Hebrews were making their brave attempts to restore their land, their holy city and their Temple. Both books are short and can be read as a whole. There are several lists of names in both books, and these may well be skipped.

It is a pity that some of the apocryphal books which appear in all Catholic Bibles are not included in other editions. This is particularly true of the book called First Maccabees. It was written early in the first century before Christ and

ecords that glorious chapter in Jewish history in which the
ation, after four hundred and fifty years of subjugation,
gain wins its religious freedom and finally, in the year 141
s.c., its political freedom. It would richly repay you to se-
ure a copy of the Bible containing the apocryphal books or
a separate copy of the Apocrypha and read this uplifting tale.
t will bring the narrative almost down to the time of Jesus,
without too many gaps, and round out the long saga of pre-
Christian Hebrew history with a fittingly triumphant close.

From the dim beginnings of the Abraham legend to the
valiant revolt of the Maccabees is a long road of history. The
Bible spans these two thousand years in sixteen books, some
ong, some brief. By following the instructions outlined
here, or reading a version of the Bible where the editor has
done the necessary cutting for you, you inherit this richly
woven story in its most appealing form.

The men and women in these narratives have become sym-
bolic figures in our civilization. Here is that mighty man of
valor, Joshua. Here are Abraham, Jacob, Elijah, Samson,
Gideon, David and his friend Jonathan, and that galaxy of
noble women: Ruth and Naomi, Rebekah, the Queen of
Sheba. And of course there are those most famous of scarlet
women, Rahab, Delilah, Bathsheba and the scheming Jezebel, all of whom remind us that the Bible does not present
us only with noble characters but with those, too, who are
"of the earth earthy." All this reading is part of your heritage, part of your gift from the past. To ignore it is to disinherit yourself of much that is best in our civilization.

The only strictly historical book in the New Testament is
the book of The Acts of the Apostles. For the Christian
reader the events in this book will seem a little nearer home.

They concern people whose names are more familiar, an
their events occur in more recent historical times. Luke, th
author of The Acts, builds his story around outstanding cha
acters rather than around dates or institutions. In this h
takes his cue from Old Testament writers.

The Acts is marked by even a greater spiritual enthusiasn
than is the historical writing of the Old Testament. As on
writer says of this book, "the fervent devotion, the daring en
durance, the missionary zeal, are not matters of statistica
reports, but of life passions of those who threw their live
away for their Christ."

The Acts requires about thirty-five pages in most moder
Bibles. Who would stop at reading thirty-five pages of a his
torical novel in an evening? Yet The Acts is more exciting
than the best historical novel. It reports an actual period i
the world's history which is reported nowhere else. It is, ir
newspaper parlance, the greatest scoop in the history of re
porting. Take this episode where Paul's nephew overhear
men plotting to take Paul's life after the apostle has beer
taken into protective custody by the Roman tribune. The
conspirators are fellow Jews who fear and hate Paul for hi
preaching of the revolutionary doctrines of Jesus Christ.

When it was day, the Jews made a plot and bound themselves by an oath neither to eat nor drink till they had killed
Paul. There were more than forty who made this conspir-
acy. And they went to the chief priests and elders, and said,
"We have strictly bound ourselves by an oath to taste no
food till we have killed Paul. You therefore, along with the
council, give notice now to the tribune to bring him down
to you, as though you were going to determine his case more
exactly. And we are ready to kill him before he comes near."
Now the son of Paul's sister heard of their ambush; so he
went and entered the barracks and told Paul. And Paul
called one of the centurions and said, "Bring this young man

to the tribune; for he has something to tell him." So he took him and brought him to the tribune and said, "Paul the prisoner called me and asked me to bring this young man to you, as he has something to say to you." The tribune took him by the hand, and going aside asked him privately, "What is it that you have to tell me?" And he said, "The Jews have agreed to ask you to bring Paul down to the council tomorrow, as though they were going to inquire somewhat more closely about him. But do not yield to them; for more than forty of their men lie in ambush for him, having bound themselves by an oath neither to eat nor drink till they have killed him; and now they are ready, waiting for the promise from you." So the tribune dismissed the young man, charging him, "Tell no one that you have informed me of this."

Then he called two of the centurions and said, "At the third hour of the night get ready two hundred soldiers with seventy horsemen and two hundred spearmen to go as far as Caesarea. Also provide mounts for Paul to ride, and bring him safely to Felix the governor." And he wrote a letter to this effect:

"Claudius Lysias to his Excellency the governor Felix, greeting. This man was seized by the Jews, and was about to be killed by them, when I came upon them with the soldiers and rescued him, having learned that he was a Roman citizen. And desiring to know the charge on which they accused him, I brought him down to their council. I found that he was accused about questions of their law, but charged with nothing deserving death or imprisonment. And when it was disclosed to me that there would be a plot against the man, I sent him to you at once, ordering his accusers also to state before you what they have against him."

So the soldiers, according to their instructions, took Paul and brought him by night to Antipatris. . . .

But the episode doesn't end there. Felix the governor guards Paul closely until he can hear the charges of the Jews against him. Five days later the high priest of the Jews and some elders and a spokesman, come to lay their case against

Paul before the governor. They call him an agitator among all the Jews and a ringleader of the sect of the Nazarenes. Felix permits Paul to speak in his own defense, which he does eloquently and brilliantly. But Felix, running true to the methods of many Roman governors, decides to keep Paul locked up until Paul can find money to buy his freedom.

The book of The Acts goes on to describe how Paul waits in prison for two years, until Felix is succeeded by another governor and how Paul is once more forced to defend himself against the charges of his fellow Jews, this time with far different results.

Chapter 14

The Great Men of God

FTER THE historical books, the largest group of writings in ne Old Testament are the books of the prophets. Just what a prophet? The word itself in its original Greek means ne who "speaks in behalf of." The prophets spoke in be- alf of God. This is different from the meaning so often at- ached exclusively to the word today, as one who can foresee ne future.

The prophets did sometimes speak of the future, especially ature punishment and reward, but their main interest was n warning and guiding their fellow men in the present. Al- ough some at times had experienced visions, they were not isionaries in the impractical sense. Their observations took oot from the life around them. They were realistic thinkers.

Many of the prophets might have been reluctant to fulfill neir appointed task of delivering God's messages, but they ad no choice. They had felt the hand of God upon them, electing them and pointing to the way they must travel. They felt possessed by God's will and message, responsible or making it clear.

The prophets were in part the conscience and scourge of ne Hebrews. They were gadflies on the body social. The Hebrews had developed the strictest and loftiest moral code nown up to their day but, like men everywhere, had diffi- ulty making it stick. The prophets were there to help them.

The Hebrew idea of history—the hand of God making it self felt in every event—gave the prophets their greatest talk ing point. God, the prophets said again and again, had shown special favor to the Hebrews by delivering them from Egyptian bondage that they might serve him. He had done his part by them; now it was up to them to repay him. If they did not, warned the prophets, God would bring disaster just as surely as stormclouds bring rain.

In Amos, the first of the prophets to write down his words we find these threatening phrases directed against his coun trymen. Notice how Amos speaks not in his own name but in the name of the Lord who has inspired him. This is true of almost all the prophets.

> Hear this word that the Lord has spoken against you, O
>   people of Israel,
> Against the whole family which I brought up out of the
>   land of Egypt:
> "You only have I known of all the families of the earth:
> Therefore I will punish you for all your iniquities. . . ."

Just as a skilled musician finds the right harmonies on his instrument, Amos plays on the fears of his listeners. He knows how to terrify them with his talk of doom and disaster. The Hebrews believed in their hearts that their sins would be punished, and this explains the power the prophets had over them. Although they were wayward, sinful and un heeding, they never forgot that Amos was right.

Tradition classifies the prophetic books under two cate gories: the major and the minor prophets. Actually these designations signify only the length of the books, not the im portance of the message. Isaiah, Jeremiah and Ezekiel, the three most prolific of the "writing prophets" are called "major." The other twelve are "minor."

To understand the prophets, it is best to read them in the

order of their appearance in time, rather than in the helter-
kelter order found in the Bible. You can only understand
them if you know in what times they were speaking, for their
words were always provoked by events then transpiring.

The prophets fall into four groups, representing roughly
four centuries.

The first group of prophets lived in the eighth century before Christ. This was the golden age of prophecy, the times
of Amos, Hosea, Micah and the man we call First Isaiah.
Here is what was happening to the little country in their
times.

The kingdom had been split into two halves, the land of
Israel to the north and Judah to the south. The Assyrian
empire was expanding rapidly through its policy of military
conquest. The Hebrews were casting frightened glances at
this colossus to the east, and with reason. Only twenty-eight
years after the appearance of Amos, the first of these prophets, the little northern kingdom was gobbled up by the Assyrians. The southern kingdom kept a toe hold on freedom
by paying fantastic sums as tribute to the Assyrians. At one
point they had to scrape the gold leaf off the walls and doors
of the Temple to make up the necessary weight of gold for
tribute.

As you read the words of the first four prophets, try to
imagine the years of suspense and upheaval in which they
lived. No man knew whether the coming year would see him
slave or free, dead or alive. Only the prophets lifted their
voices with faith and certainty in those years. Only the
prophets believed that freedom and righteousness would prevail, so long as the Hebrews walked uprightly in the way of
their Lord.

Amos. Amos' prophetic words burst like a whirlwind on

the Hebrews of the northern kingdom in a critical period
It was shortly before the coming Assyrian invasion. At the
time a generation had grown up in Israel which had no
known war. Such unpleasant things were forgotten during
the days of a new commercial prosperity.

But this prosperity brought much evil and social injustice
with it. Wealth was in the hands of a few. Luxury, vice
corruption were everywhere. Here is what Amos said:

> Thus says the Lord:
> "For three transgressions of Israel
> And for four, I will not revoke the punishment;
> Because they sell the righteous for silver,
> And the needy for a pair of shoes—
> They that trample the head of the poor into the dust of
>   the earth,
> And turn aside the way of the afflicted . . .
> They lay themselves down beside every altar
> Upon garments taken in pledge;
> And in the house of their God they drink
> The wine of those who have been fined."

Amos also objected to the way his countrymen relied upon
the empty observance of ritual, thinking thereby to secure
the Lord's forgiveness for their sins:

> Therefore thus says the Lord . . .
> "I hate, I despise your feasts,
> And I take no delight in your solemn assemblies.
> Even though you offer me your burnt offerings and
>   cereal offerings,
> I will not accept them,
> And the peace offerings of your fatted beasts
> I will not look upon.
> Take away from me the noise of your songs;
> To the melody of your harps I will not listen.
> But let justice roll down like waters,
> And righteousness like an overflowing stream."

The last two lines reveal the greatness of Amos' message.
And it is typical of the inspiration of all the prophets. The
prophets seem to live on mountain peaks, on the highest sum-
mits of human thought. Somehow they knew what was honest and right and true, and found the courage to say it. And
it usually required courage. Fault-finders have never been
popular, and those who came in the name of the Lord, backed
up by his immense authority, as they repeatedly declared,
were bound to be even less popular than most. The Hebrews
might listen to their prophets and in their hearts agree with
them, but almost certainly avoided any human contact with
them when possible. The prophets staked out lonely lives
for themselves because they would not share the mediocrities
and compromises of the great mass of people. Although you
may find their stubbornness and singlemindedness trying,
you cannot fail to admire them. When have men ever made
progress without voices like these to warn them and point
out the paths they should take?

Hosea. Hosea appeared within ten years after Amos had
left the northern cities. His manner is much milder than
that of Amos. He prefers persuasion to outright condemna-
tion and stresses God's love rather than his revenge. In these
beautiful words of the eleventh chapter, he speaks for God
about the coming doom of the kingdom, but ends with God's
announcement of mercy for his special people. Notice that
when Hosea speaks of Ephraim, he is referring to the northern kingdom, Israel; the section known as Ephraim was the
nucleus of that country.

> When Israel was a child, I loved him,
> And out of Egypt I called my son . . .
> Yet it was I who taught Ephraim to walk,
> I took them up in my arms;

But they did not know that I healed them.
I led them with cords of compassion,
With the bands of love,
And I became to them as one
Who eases the yoke on their jaws,
And I bent down to them and fed them.

They shall return to the land of Egypt,
And Assyria shall be their king,
Because they have refused to return to me.
The sword shall rage against their cities,
Consume the bars of their gates,
And devour them in their fortresses . . .

How can I give you up, O Ephraim!
How can I hand you over, O Israel! . . .
My heart recoils within me,
My compassion grows warm and tender.
I will not execute my fierce anger,
I will not again destroy Ephraim;
For I am God and not man,
The Holy One in your midst,
And I will not come to destroy.

However, Hosea is capable of great anger in the name of the Lord, and in the thirteenth chapter lets loose a word-lashing that must have made his listeners shake in their shoes. Furious because the Hebrews have forgotten him, the Lord decrees his punishment in these harsh words:

So I will be to them like a lion,
Like a leopard I will lurk beside the way.
I will fall upon them like a bear robbed of her cubs,
I will tear open their breast,
And there I will devour them like a lion,
As a wild beast would rend them.

I will destroy you, O Israel;
Who can help you?

At the close, Hosea once more holds out the Lord's gracious and tender promise that he will love his people freely if they will return to him and dwell beneath his shadow.

Micah. When Micah comes on the scene the northern kingdom is on the verge of destruction. The southern kingdom of Judah is threatened, but so far has escaped destruction. Now Micah comes from his outlying country village to tell of his vision of the coming fall of both kingdoms. He has seen evil in the treatment of farmers by the city landlords:

> They covet fields, and seize them;
> And houses, and take them away;
> They oppress a man and his house,
> A man and his inheritance.

In high prophetic style, Micah thunders in the Lord's name that doom is coming, from which they shall not remove their necks. He sees corruption in high places, saying of the rulers of Jerusalem that they

> . . . give judgment for a bribe,
> Its priests teach for hire,
> Its prophets divine for money . . .

and warns that because of this,

> Zion shall be plowed as a field;
> Jerusalem shall become a heap of ruins,
> And the mountain of the house a wooded height.

But Micah does more than point the finger of accusation and cry for justice. He has had a vision, a great vision. He sees a time of universal peace and brotherhood to come, when goodness shall at last prevail on earth and evil will evaporate like the mountain dew. This magnificent vision occupies the central portion of the book of Micah, beginning with Chapter 4. Here are the solemn, soaring words with which it starts:

> It shall come to pass in the latter days
> That the mountain of the house of the Lord
> Shall be established as the highest of the mountains,
> And shall be raised up above the hills;
> And peoples shall flow to it,
> And many nations shall come, and say:
> "Come let us go up to the mountain of the Lord,
> To the house of the God of Jacob;
> That he may teach us his ways
> And we may walk in his paths."
> For out of Zion shall go forth the law,
> And the word of the Lord from Jerusalem.
> He shall judge between many peoples,
> And shall decide for strong nations afar off;
> And they shall beat their swords into plowshares,
> And their spears into pruning hooks;
> Nation shall not lift up sword against nation,
> Neither shall they learn war any more;
> But they shall sit every man under his vine and un-
>   der his fig tree,
> And none shall make them afraid;
> For the mouth of the Lord of hosts has spoken.

This is the vision of a great poet and a great soul. So treasured was it that it is found repeated almost verbatim in the
opening verses of the second chapter of Isaiah. Try reading
it aloud to see how the words ring out and fill your heart.

Isaiah. Isaiah is usually considered the greatest of the
prophets. He lived and preached in the most critical times
of all: from about 740 B.C. to 701 B.C. Year after year he saw
the Assyrian armies plucking off the surrounding cities like
ripe fruit. He saw the inevitable circle narrow to his own beloved country, and finally to his own city of Jerusalem. But

Isaiah was a great man, with a stony courage and an unblinking faith that could tide him through the bitterest times. In the closing circle of ruin and desolation, his confidence in God never left him. If his country was to be destroyed, it was part of God's greater plan.

The Assyrians were a rod in the hand of God to punish the Hebrews for their iniquities; but after his will was done in Jerusalem, he would in turn punish the pride and arrogance of the king of Assyria.

Isaiah attempts to calm any lingering doubts that this is the Lord's plan and within his power. Although the Assyrians are now the rod of God's wrath against the Hebrews, God retains full control over their actions:

> Shall the ax vaunt itself over him who hews with it,
> Or the saw magnify itself against him who wields it?
> As if a rod should wield him who lifts it,
> Or as if a staff should lift him who is not wood!
> Therefore the Lord, the Lord of hosts,
> Will send wasting sickness among his stout warriors,
> And under his glory a burning will be kindled,
> Like the burning of fire.
> The light of Israel will become a fire,
> And his Holy One a flame.

Aside from reading the book of Isaiah for its mighty prophetical invective against the sins of the Hebrews, or for its new and larger concept of God as the creator and controller of the whole earth, you can read it as the record of a busy, practical man of affairs. Isaiah was trying to help his country find the path that would lead to continued freedom. To help him and to console him if he failed, he had his belief in God. But he also had work to do. While kings trembled and courtiers blindly plotted intrigue and treason, Isaiah gave advice, worked behind the scenes, protested against foreign negotiations and alliances. He was truly a statesman, a man of political affairs. Behind the words which we have in the book that bears his name, we feel a strong active personality doing his best to keep his country free in the face of an appalling menace.

The careful reader of Isaiah will notice that Chapters 36, 37, 38 and 39 are borrowed with some variations from chapters he has already read in II Kings. Originally dealing with the times of Isaiah, these chapters were evidently inserted here as a sort of connecting link to bind the utterances of that prophet with a matchless collection of poems composed several centuries later and comprising Chapters 40 to 66. For want of a better name, many biblical scholars call these closing chapters, "Second Isaiah." They are marked by a totally different literary style, they come from a different historical period, and the religious emphasis is markedly different from that of the early Isaiah. This closing section of the book of Isaiah constitutes one more reason why this book is considered a biblical masterpiece. These later chapters will be discussed a little farther on.

Zephaniah. The second group of prophets, Nahum, Habakkuk, Zephaniah and Jeremiah, lived approximately a century later than the group just discussed. By this time the northern kingdom had fallen to the Assyrians—in 722 B.C. Shortly thereafter, in the reign of the Assyrian Sennacherib, the southern nation had miraculously escaped extinction, as recorded in Isaiah, Chapters 36 and 37. An Assyrian army had come and camped outside the gates of Jerusalem but a strange plague had struck them and decimated their numbers. A century of truce followed, when the Hebrews managed to buy their freedom with tribute money. This truce was followed in 627 B.C. by an invasion of the savage tribe of Scythians which led the grim prophet Zephaniah to declare that the day of doom for all nations had come. His fears were unrealized, but in expressing them he wrote some magnificent lines of poetry.

Nahum. Finally in 612 B.C. came the great news that the Assyrians had been defeated by another nation, the Babylonians, or Chaldeans, as they are sometimes called. It was naturally a joyful occasion and inspired Nahum, a poet of the time, to give us an imaginative picture of the fall of Nineveh, the Assyrian capital. His wild and savage song of triumph reminds us of Deborah's paean of triumph in the book of Judges. It is a classic of picture-evoking realism, ending with these lines:

> Your shepherds are asleep,
> O king of Assyria;
> Your nobles slumber.
> Your people are scattered on the mountains
> With none to gather them.
> There is no assuaging your hurt,
> Your wound is grievous.
> All who hear the news of you
> Clap their hands over you.
> For upon whom has not come
> Your unceasing evil?

But the rejoicing was premature. The Assyrians were cast down, but another tyranny had come to take their place. The Babylonians took upon themselves the mantle of conquest, and began to despoil the lands of their neighbors just as the Assyrians had done before them.

Habakkuk. Habakkuk hears of the Babylonian successes, and foresees the day when they will be at the gates. Here

is his vision of the approaching hordes of Babylon, words
that certainly filled his countrymen with fear:

> They all come for violence;
> Terror of them goes before them.
> They gather captives like sand.
> At kings they scoff,
> And of rulers they make sport.
> They laugh at every fortress,
> For they heap up earth and take it.
> Then they sweep by like the wind and go on,
> Guilty men, whose own might is their god!

But Habakkuk does more than foretell doom. He has a
searching question to ask the Lord, the question that must
occur to all men who place their faith in him. It is the same
question that Job was to ask. Briefly it is, "In God's plan,
why is it that the righteous suffer?"

Habakkuk poses the question in five beautiful lines:

> Thou who art of purer eyes than to behold evil
> And canst not look on wrong,
> Why dost thou look on faithless men,
> And art silent when the wicked swallows up
> The man more righteous than he?

His listeners must have held their breath as they waited
for the Lord's answer to such a question. On the answer
much depended, because this was a query each man asked
himself as the troubles of the little country mounted. Habakkuk announces,

> I will take my stand to watch,
> And station myself on the tower,
> And look forth to see what he will say to me,
> And what I will answer concerning my complaint.
> And the Lord answered me:

"Write the vision;
Make it plain upon tablets,
So he may run who reads it.
For still the vision awaits its time;
It hastens to the end—it will not lie.
If it seems slow, wait for it;
It will surely come, it will not delay.
Behold, he whose soul is not upright in him shall fail,
But the righteous shall live by his faith."

This last line is one of the profoundest declarations in the Bible: "The righteous shall live by his faith." Paul made this statement ring throughout the Roman world. Luther took it from Paul and shook Europe with its reforming power. It has been ringing ever since.

The book of Habakkuk covers only a page or two in your Bible. It can be read two or three times in less than half an hour. But in this little book you will find priceless gems of men's faith in God.

Habakkuk ends with as magnificent a burst of faith as ever a man uttered:

Though the fig tree do not blossom,
Nor fruit be on the vines,
The produce of the olive fail
And the fields yield no food,
The flock be cut off from the fold
And there be no herd in the stalls,
Yet I will rejoice in the Lord,
I will joy in the God of my salvation.

Jeremiah. The prophet Jeremiah is sometimes called "the prophet with the bleeding heart." Certainly his book, the second longest in the Bible, is one of the saddest of all, and the most genuinely personal. We feel more of the writer's true personality than we do in any other of the prophetical books. Even its lack of order and organization reflects its complete genuineness. It might almost be called the diary of a deeply religious man living through his nation's stormiest years.

For Jeremiah lived during the years that were to see the actual accomplishment of the doom that had been so long foretold. In his time the Babylonians came not once, but twice, to conquer what remained of the land. The first time Nebuchadnezzar arrived with his armies was in 597 B.C.; he took the city of Jerusalem, carried the king into captivity with him, and set up a puppet monarch of his own. When this monarch, against Jeremiah's advice, tried to rebel against the Babylonian yoke, disaster struck again. This time, eleven years later, Nebuchadnezzar returned and leveled the city. This was the beginning of the exile for most of the Hebrews. Jeremiah saw all these events.

Jeremiah's preaching of non-resistance to the Babylonians (to him the only course of action that was not national suicide) was extremely unpopular. He advised appeasement— bitter words for a proud people like the Hebrews. And he suffered for his words. He was thrown into prison. He spent seven years in hiding. He was flogged. He was put in stocks. He narrowly escaped death in an old well. But nothing could prevent the aging prophet from saying what he felt was right.

Jeremiah's advice did not stop with his practical words on foreign policy, however. Sensible policies by the government were perhaps his first and most immediate aim. But like all prophets, he also advocated that certain spiritual steps be taken to strengthen the state. He demanded that the people return to the true worship of God and forswear foreign religious practices. With his unshakeable conviction of the over-lordship of the one true God, he guaranteed that these actions would salvage their fortunes. But his people did not share his conviction.

Like all the prophets, Jeremiah makes grand, uplifting reading. Men of such faith are rare in any time, and to listen to his ironclad belief in the triumph of God is still inspiring. Although Jeremiah failed to awaken his own people spiritually, it is safe to say that he has over the centuries aroused hundreds of thousands of people to a more courageous way of life.

The next group of prophets, in point of time, were men who shared the days of exile in Babylon with their countrymen. They were Ezekiel, and the writer we know today only as "Second Isaiah."

Ezekiel. Ezekiel was taken into captivity after the first siege of Jerusalem, in 597 B.C. His book differs from most other prophetical books in that about one fourth of it consists of visions which came to him. It opens with one of these visions, which occupies the first three chapters. The most extensive of them is in Chapters 40 to 46 where he sees the plan for a new Temple which will one day rise in a rebuilt Jerusalem.

Ezekiel is in many ways a difficult book to read. But it will help if you remember the facts surrounding the Babylonian captivity of the Hebrews. It was a time when many were being weaned away from their ancestral faith. In the face of stirring new political and commercial events, they were forgetting their Temple and their law.

Ezekiel was of the priestly line of Zadok. To him there was nothing so important as to keep the remnant of his people true to their faith. We probably owe to Ezekiel more

than to any other Bible writer the preservation of the contents of the Old Testament as we have them today. Although
there was no Temple, no sacrifices, no priesthood, Ezekiel
encouraged the exiles to meet and talk of their God and his
commandments. And under the stimulus of Babylon's advanced culture, the job of writing down the history and
teachings of the past was begun. Much of the Old Testament
may have been edited and put into regular use under the
direction of Ezekiel during the busy but deadening days of
exile.

Second Isaiah. Out of this literary activity in exile came
some of the choicest new writings, notably the 40th to 66th
chapters of Isaiah. Because we do not know the author's
name and because his works were attached by later editors
to the sermons of the statesman-prophet of the eighth century, many of today's Bible commentators refer to him as
Second Isaiah. Some scholars think that the writings of the
eighth century prophet close with the 35th chapter and that
more than one later writer has contributed to Chapters 36-66.
At all events, the chief of these exilic writers, whom we call
Second Isaiah, struck a new note in prophecy. His words
are not prophetic exhortations and denunciations, but rhapsodies. They contain an exultation, a sustained ecstasy that
is unlike the works of his predecessors. One edition of the
Bible refers to the poems of this man as "The Rhapsodies of
the Unknown Prophet," and it is a good title.

The fortieth chapter of Isaiah has been called the most
beautiful literature ever penned. Its opening stanzas hold
out the hope of rescue and pardon to the captives:

> Comfort, comfort my people,
> Says your God.
> Speak tenderly to Jerusalem,

And cry to her
That her warfare is ended,
That her iniquity is pardoned,
That she has received from the Lord's hand
Double for all her sins.

A voice cries:
"In the wilderness prepare the way of the Lord,
Make straight in the desert a highway for our God.
Every valley shall be lifted up,
And every mountain and hill be made low;
The uneven ground shall become level,
And the rough places a plain.
And the glory of the Lord shall be revealed,
And all flesh shall see it together,
For the mouth of the Lord has spoken."

But behind the emotion of the words lies something more significant. It is from this and the chapters following that there emerges the full-robed picture of God. He is no longer simply Jehovah, the God of the Hebrews, but suddenly the God of all mankind. This is the God we meet in the New Testament. Later in Chapter 40 we read these majestic words:

Have you not known? Have you not heard?
Has it not been told you from the beginning?
Have you not understood from the foundations of the earth?
It is he who sits above the circle of the earth,
And its inhabitants are like grasshoppers;
Who stretches out the heavens like a curtain,
And spreads them like a tent to dwell in;
Who brings princes to nought,
And makes the rulers of the earth as nothing.

It was also to Chapter 40 of Isaiah that each of the four gospel writers went to explain the coming of Christ. Indeed nowhere in the Old Testament do we find ourselves breathing so much of the air of the New as in Second Isaiah. In

Chapter 53 we find one of the many, and probably the best known, references to the "servant" who shall one day atone for the sins of the world. Here we are very close to Christianity:

> Surely he has borne our griefs
> And carried our sorrows . . .
> But he was wounded for our transgressions,
> He was bruised for our iniquities;
> Upon him was the chastisement that made us whole,
> And with his stripes we are healed.
> All we like sheep have gone astray;
> We have turned every one to his own way;
> And the Lord has laid on him
> The iniquity of us all.

It is obvious in the New Testament that nothing in the ancient Jewish scriptures meant more to the first Christians than the closing chapters of the book of Isaiah. The most dramatic incident was recorded by Luke when Jesus himself, invited to read the scriptures at the synagogue service in his home town of Nazareth, turned to the 61st chapter, read its opening verses. . . .

> The Spirit of the Lord God is upon me,
> Because the Lord has anointed me
> To bring good tidings to the afflicted;
> He has sent me to bind up the broken-hearted,
> To proclaim liberty to the captives,
> And the opening of the prison to those who are bound;
> To proclaim the year of the Lord's favor . . .

. . . closed the book and said, "Today this scripture has been fulfilled in your hearing."

Second Isaiah is clearly the bridge between the Old and New Testaments. But at the time his words were written, during the exile in Babylon, they must have had a great effect on his hearers. Without doubt some Hebrews were encouraged by this poetry and found in it consolation for the loss of their country and homes. It is typical of the religious genius of the Hebrew people that here in their darkest hour the brightest fire of the Old Testament was kindled.

The fourth and last group of prophets lived in the years just following the return from Babylon, and they can only be understood in reference to these times. It was an epoch of great dejection. The people had come close to losing all faith in the religion of their fathers. They lacked energy even to hew a new Temple. The country was overrun with hostile strangers.

Haggai and Zechariah. In this period, the prophet Haggai preached four sermons to inspire the people to rebuild the Temple. He has been called the prophet of "stones and timber" because his brief messages dealt mainly with rebuilding. Zechariah, a contemporary of Haggai, who helped him spur the people onward, clothed his message in striking visions and symbols.

Obadiah. Obadiah, who has the distinction of having written the shortest book in the Old Testament, cries out for vengeance on the neighboring land of Edom, Israel's ancient enemy. He is angry with them for not having come to the assistance of the Hebrews in their struggle with Babylon. Says Obadiah,

On the day that you stood aloof,
On the day that strangers carried off his wealth,
And foreigners entered his gates
And cast lots for Jerusalem,
You were like one of them.

But you should not have gloated over the day of your brother
In the day of his misfortune;
You should not have rejoiced over the people of Judah
In the day of their ruin;
You should not have boasted
In the day of distress.

Malachi. Malachi is not a proper name but means "my
messenger" and is derived from the mysterious "messenger"
in the first verse of the third chapter. The author's name is
not known, but he was apparently a contemporary of Obadiah. In the book of Malachi, the intuitive flashes of the
earlier prophets are replaced by a more logical question-and-
answer discussion of religious problems. He speaks in cold,
precise prose, not in the fiery verse of his predecessors. And
yet this author has his memorable moments. In these lines
he tried to strengthen men's faith in discouraging times:

For from the rising of the sun to its setting my name is great
among the nations, and in every place incense is offered to
my name, and a pure offering; for my name is great among
the nations, says the Lord of hosts.

He also wrote these well-known lines in the second chapter.

Have we not all one father? Has not one God created us?
Why then are we faithless to one another?

Joel. From some unnamed day of terror in Israel's tragic
history when a cloud of locusts swept through the land, eating the leaves from the trees, invading the houses and shaving
the grass from the fields, Joel drew an analogy to the dreadful
Judgment Day of the Lord. No one seems to know the date
of his writing. But like almost all the prophets, this book is
not without its ray of hope. The book ends:

Egypt shall become a desolation
And Edom a desolate wilderness,
For the violence done the people of Judah,
Because they have shed innocent blood in their land.
But Judah shall be inhabited for ever,
And Jerusalem to all generations.
I will avenge their blood and I will not clear the guilty,
For the Lord dwells in Zion.

Jonah. The book of Jonah, though listed with the prophets, is quite unlike any other prophetic book. It is not fiery
verse but a tale of protest. Jonah is a narrow-minded lay
preacher, no doubt intended by the author of the story to
represent some of the narrow-minded members of the Jewish
clergy of his time. He is directed by the Lord to do some
missionary work in the city of Nineveh. This Jonah refuses
to do since he considers that Assyrian city the wickedest
place on earth, and a fit candidate for destruction. So he
takes a ship going in the opposite direction, toward Spain,
in fact.

The Lord pursues him, arranges for him to be forcibly
ejected from the ship and frees him from the belly of the
great fish which has swallowed him, only after Jonah has
repented his behavior.

Once there, Jonah preaches the coming anger of the Lord
against the city: "Yet forty days," he cries out, "and Nineveh
shall be overthrown!" The people are deeply moved by his
words and experience a genuine change of heart. The Lord,
seeing this change, decides against punishing them after all.

And now comes the slightly comical twist to the tale.
Jonah becomes extremely angry with God when he finds that
the city is not to be destroyed. He does not want to share
his God, gracious and merciful, and his religion, with a

heathen city. He prefers that the city be destroyed regardless of its new awakening.

But the Lord rebukes Jonah for his selfishness. He makes it abundantly clear that he cares deeply for every city, even so pagan a one as Nineveh.

A word here about the translation of the Bible you select for reading the prophets. Many readers have found, since the publication in 1952 of the Old Testament in the Revised Standard Version, that this translation most quickly unlocks the meaning of the prophets. The style of these men is highly literary, full of ornate images, metaphors, and sweeping stairs of parallel sentences. When these forms are cast in the involved and unfamiliar language of the King James Version, it tends to increase the reading difficulties. Some passages are complicated enough without adding to them the obscurities of English prose that is three and a half centuries old. With this in mind, all selections from the prophets quoted in the foregoing section have been taken from the Revised Standard Version.

Other readers, however, stoutly declare that to be unfamiliar with the prophetical books in the stirring language of the King James Version is to disinherit yourself voluntarily from a great literary treasure. There is some truth in this. The ideal solution, perhaps, is to use several translations, comparing their beauty and clarity in all your favorite passages.

Chapter 15

A Golden Treasury of Great Writing

THE WRITINGS, as distinct from the Law and the Prophets, consist of these thirteen books: Psalms, Proverbs, Job, Song of Solomon, Ruth, Lamentations, Ecclesiastes, Esther, Daniel, Ezra, Nehemiah, and I and II Chronicles. These books are of five types—history, poetry, drama, philosophy and stories of people. Although the Writings differ from one another in time of composition, style and content—as much, for example, as the works of Chaucer, Shakespeare and Charles Dickens—they are all knit through with the golden thread which binds the whole Bible together. Each one deals, in its own fashion, with man's relationship to God. Nothing interested thoughtful Hebrews more, and nothing turned up more often in their literature.

We have already mentioned the four books among the Writings which deal with historical events: I and II Chronicles, Ezra and Nehemiah. The present chapter deals with the other books among the Writings.

The books of Ruth, Esther, and the first six chapters of Daniel are examples of the most popular kind of writing—stories about people. Each was apparently written for a definite purpose.

Ruth. The book of Ruth was probably written in the fourth century B.C., in the days following the return from the exile. Strict decrees forbidding the marriage of Hebrews with foreigners had been promulgated some time earlier. These laws were passed by Nehemiah, the governor, who was afraid that the tiny band of returned Jews would lose their racial identity by marrying with the various non-Jewish strains then occupying the land. Theoretically, the law might perhaps be justifiable, but in practice it must have led to some heart-breaking situations. It forced Jewish men already married to foreign wives to divorce them.

The author of Ruth took up his pen to show that the laws were cruel and unfair. He tells of a girl who lived in the far-off time of the Judges, before the time of King Saul and King David. She was a foreigner, a girl of Moab, but a fine, loyal, generous person. She has the chance to stay in her native land, but because she has married the son of a Hebrew couple, decides, when her husband and father-in-law both die, to accompany her mother-in-law back to Israel. Her mother-in-law, Naomi, urges her to stay among her own people, but Ruth replies,

> Intreat me not to leave thee, or to return from following after thee, for whither thou goest, I will go; and where thou lodgest, I will lodge: thy people shall be my people, and thy God my God; where thou diest, will I die, and there will I be buried: the Lord do so to me, and more also, if ought but death part thee and me.

These words must have echoed the pleas of the foreign wives who were separated by law from the men they loved.

The author makes his point very gently. Ruth, the foreigner, wins the love of a good man in her adopted land, and bears him a son destined to become the grandfather of King David. Therefore, the author is saying, "If our great and beloved King David came from foreign stock, what harm could such intermarriage do to any of us?"

Few works of protest have been written in as tender and appealing a way as the book of Ruth. And because it is so gently written, its message of tolerance has been largely forgotten while people read it as the romantic story it also is.

Daniel. The first six chapters of the book of Daniel seem to have been written to encourage the people in their struggle against the religious persecutions of the Syrian king, Antiochus Epiphanes, in the second century, B.C. He was trying to force Greek culture and religion on Palestine and to eradicate all traces of Judaism. Daniel is the hero, not the author of these chapters, a Jew who stood up to the tyranny of Babylon and Persia in a much earlier time. As the Jews read this gripping story, no doubt circulated illegally and speaking only metaphorically of their own situation, they must have taken heart. The story of a man and his companions who rose above the oppression of a foreign king with their faith intact and their lives spared had a message for their own day.

Esther. The last of the short stories of the Old Testament is the book of Esther. This is the only book of the Bible which does not once mention the name of God. It was written by an unknown author in Jerusalem, probably as late as 125 B.C. Its heroine is a beautiful Jewish girl who rose to become Queen of Persia, then risked her life to save her people. This book was evidently written to give the background of the newly introduced holiday, the Feast of Purim. Doubtless starting as a popular tale, the story of Esther came to be so closely associated with the Jewish Feast of Purim that when the time came to decide on its place in the holy canon, it was included.

Psalms. The book of Psalms is probably the most familiar of the Writings of the Bible. Tradition has it that David himself poured out these noble lines. Wasn't he a musician, strumming melodies on his harp to sooth the tired Saul? Wasn't he a dancer, leaping and dancing before the Ark of the Lord after its recapture from the Philistines? How natural for the legend to grow that this warrior with the soul of an artist was the composer of most of the beautiful Psalms.

But actually the book of Psalms, as indicated by several of the headings, is an anthology of hymns by many poets, not the collected works of one. David may have had a hand in some, but even this is not certain. Some were written after the return from exile, more than six centuries after David.

If David was not the psalmist, who was? Look at the poems closely and you will sometimes be able to see for yourself. All kinds of people opened their hearts in these poems: shepherds, farmers, priests and pious citizens. Only a man to whom the shepherd's life was familiar could have written the beautiful Twenty-third Psalm, beginning, "The Lord is my shepherd; I shall not want." Perhaps a shepherd poet composed the first version of such lines as these from the Eighth Psalm:

> When I consider thy heavens, the work of thy fingers,
> The moon and the stars, which thou hast ordained;
> What is man, that thou art mindful of him?
> And the son of man, that thou visitest him?

Among the psalmists there must have been pious Jews who wrote not "for publication," not thoughts to be aired in the great religious services, but only to be read by themselves and their families at home. Psalm 51 is one of these personal expressions. We can hear a sincere and pious man, saying in the privacy of his home:

> Create in me a clean heart, O God;
> And renew a right spirit within me.
> Cast me not away from thy presence;
> And take not thy holy spirit from me.

Certainly some psalmists were priests, interested in finding new ways to express the religious spirit that moved them. But these were not cloistered men. They undoubtedly knew and loved their country. Perhaps a priest, searching for a new way to tell his congregation of his love for God, wrote,

> As the hart panteth after the water brooks,
> So panteth my soul after thee, O God.

As you read the Psalms, you will have definite impressions about the authorship of different ones. Trust these feelings. Scholars have little definite information about the authors, and your own surmises will help make your reading more rewarding.

In the American Standard Version and the Revised Standard Version of the Bible, the Psalms are divided into five books ending in order with numbers 41, 72, 89, 106 and 150. Each of these five books is a collection of Psalms made at some point in Hebrew history. Each book ends with a sort of benediction, with Psalm 150 as a fitting close for them all.

Our purpose is not to call attention here to all the beauties of the Psalms. Exploring among them is one of the great pleasures of reading the Bible. A good place to begin your browsing is with numbers 1, 19, 23, 24, 46, 90, 103 and 121. Over the centuries, these Psalms have won the most devotees. Because each poem is so charged with meaning, it is difficult to read more than a few at a single sitting. They are most profitably read along with other parts of the Bible.

Psalm 119 presents some interesting features. The longest chapter in the Bible, it is an acrostic divided into twenty-two stanzas of eight lines each. In the original language, the first word in each line of each stanza begins with a letter of the Hebrew alphabet in order. Thus, the first letter of each line of the first eight verses begins in Hebrew with the first letter of the alphabet, "aleph." Another feature of this remarkable poem is that every one of its 176 verses is a tribute to the Word of God. The Word is given many names: law, testimonies, ways, precepts, statutes, commandments and ordinances.

This Psalm also offers an excellent example of the structure of Hebrew poetry. Where we distinguish most of our poetic expression in English by its syllabic rhythm and often by its phonetic rhyme, the Hebrew poet usually attains his effect by repeating his thought in successive lines, but with different words. This is called "parallelism." In the song of Deborah in the book of Judges, probably the oldest passage in the Bible, a striking example of this poetic form occurs. Exulting over the death of Sisera, the Canaanite chief, Deborah sings:

At her feet he bowed, he fell, he lay down:
At her feet he bowed, he fell:
Where he bowed, there he fell down dead.

Here is a good example of parallelism in the 103rd verse of Psalm 119:

How sweet are thy words to my taste,
Sweeter than honey to my mouth.

Many examples can also be found in the prophets, as in the closing lines of the fortieth chapter of Isaiah:

But they who wait for the Lord shall renew their strength,
They shall mount up with wings like eagles,
They shall run and not be weary,
They shall walk and not faint.

Job. The book of Job is the only full-scale drama in the Bible. Because most of our English Bibles are not printed so that the reader can easily distinguish between prose and poetry, readers are often unaware that while the first two chapters comprise a prose prologue and the closing verses of the last chapter, a prose epilogue, the rest is poetry. The theme is the ever-present one, also voiced by Habakkuk: "Why do the righteous suffer?"

And again the question receives the same answer—we must live by faith. Faith does not demand an explanation for every experience on earth or for the existence of evil. Faith puts its trust in God's love and care.

There is very little in the world's literature to compare with the intense rhetoric of the author of Job. It overwhelms the reader with its imagery, its wealth of symbols, its sustained dramatic feeling. It rushes on and on in deepening intensity and eloquence. It can be read and reread, like all great literature, without tiring you.

The climax of the drama comes in God's rebuke to Job, which begins with the first verse of Chapter 38. Job has pointed out that he has led a blameless, dutiful and God-fearing life and yet has been visited with disaster. Where is the justice of this, he wants to know. With the challenge, "Behold my desire is, that the Almighty would answer me," Job puts his question up to God.

In the poems of Chapters 38, 39 and 40, the Lord answers Job "out of the whirlwind." By a series of gigantic questions, which Job is unable to answer, God demonstrates that he alone can make plans for man and the universe, and that no man can hope to understand his way of justice. The faltering mind of man can never grasp the vast outlines of divine judgment.

Where were you when I laid the foundation of the earth?
Tell me, if you have understanding.
Who determined its measurements—surely you know!
Or who stretched the line upon it?
On what were its bases sunk,
Or who laid its cornerstone,
When the morning stars sang together,
And all the sons of God shouted for joy?

Or who shut in the sea with doors,
When it burst forth from the womb;
When I made clouds its garment,
And thick darkness its swaddling band,
And prescribed bounds for it,
And set bars and doors,
And said, "Thus far shall you come, and no farther,
And here shall your proud waves be stayed"?

Question after question adds to the proof of God's power.
On what grounds, then, does Job condemn God? How can
he presume to doubt divine justice? And at last Job admits
that he was wrong to have doubted God's plan, although powerless to discern its beginning and end. The proof that there
is such a plan is too great to question. Job has experienced
the presence of God, and that is satisfaction enough. At the
close of the drama, he bows his head and declares,

Therefore I have uttered what I did not understand,
Things too wonderful for me, which I did not know . . .
I had heard of thee by the hearing of the ear,
But now my eye sees thee;
Therefore I despise myself
And repent in dust and ashes.

The book of Job gives us almost no clue as to when it was
composed. Most scholars date it about 400 B.C., some years
after the return from exile. We know next to nothing about
the man who wrote this book, beyond the fact that he was
certainly an inspired writer, and gave us a lyric textbook of

faith that must be ranked in any catalogue as one of the world's supreme literary achievements.

Song of Solomon. The Song of Solomon, although attributed by its title to Solomon, is not definitely of his authorship. Most scholars believe that it was written by a Hebrew very much taken with the literary styles of Egypt or Persia, because of its many references to doves, gazelles, foreign fruits and spices and lavish gardens. The restraint of traditional Hebrew writing is lacking, as the writer sings with rapture of the love between man and woman.

The Song of Solomon is also regarded by some scholars as a drama, for in it different persons (although not named) seem to participate. By others it is considered the only purely lyric poetry in the Bible. No reader can fail to be stirred by the sheer beauty of many of its lines.

> Arise, my love, my fair one,
> And come away;
> For lo, the winter is past,
> The rain is over and gone.
> The flowers appear on the earth,
> The time of singing has come,
> And the voice of the turtledove
> Is heard in our land.
> The fig tree puts forth its figs,
> And the vines are in blossom;
> They give forth fragrance.
> Arise, my love, my fair one,
> And come away.
> O my dove, in the clefts of the rock,
> In the covert of the cliff,
> Let me see your face,
> Let me hear your voice,
> For your voice is sweet,
> And your face is comely.

Lamentations. The book of Lamentations is probably the least read book of the Bible. It is a collection of dirges, and most readers do not feel attracted to their message of despair. It stems from the occasion of the fall of Jerusalem to the Babylonians, and is attributed (though not in the Hebrew) to Jeremiah who was present on the day the city fell.

Those readers who are familiar with the agonies through which the Jewish people have passed in ancient, medieval and modern times will find an early echo of it in this long poem.

Proverbs. Just as the people who hero-worshiped David gave him credit for writing the book of Psalms, the people who revered Solomon's wisdom assign him as author of the book of Proverbs. However, they were scarcely justified in doing so. Modern scholars think that Proverbs contains almost nothing of Solomon's personal thoughts. The Proverbs seem to date from a later period, when the intellectual life of the nation was more subtle and self-conscious. Back in the tenth century, in the days of Solomon, the nation was younger and more vigorous. The artificial style of proverb writing had not yet developed.

The book of Proverbs is a little library of wise and witty sayings. They are so sharp and concentrated that it is hard to read more than a few at one time with full attention. However, they provide food for thought for hours. Some people choose one or two proverbs to read every morning before leaving for work, knowing that their sound and salty advice can often get them off to a good start.

The book is a collection of several writers' work, made up of eight different collections of proverbs that were in circulation around 400 B.C. The original collections were culled from the wisdom of wise men, or sages, some of whom are mentioned by name. Many of these wise men were teachers, anxious to pass on to their young students brief maxims about the life ahead of them. Some have a familiar ring. What youngster hasn't had the busy ant held up as a model of industry and perseverance? In Proverbs we come across the same ants, this time being praised like this:

> Go to the ant, O sluggard;
> Consider her ways and be wise.
> Without having any chief,
> Officer or ruler,
> She prepares her food in summer,
> And gathers her sustenance in harvest.
> How long will you lie there, O sluggard?
> When will you arise from your sleep?
> A little sleep, a little slumber,
> A little folding of the hands to rest,
> And poverty will come upon you like a vagabond,
> And want like an armed man.

Each writer probably took enormous and justifiable pride in his collection of proverbs and spent many hours whittling them into briefer and wittier form. Our book of Proverbs is made up of these jewel-like phrases, written by many men over a period of perhaps five hundred years.

Ecclesiastes. Like Proverbs, the book of Ecclesiastes belongs to a type of literature found among all the ancients and called wisdom literature, the work of sages and philosophers.

However, Ecclesiastes is not a collection of sayings, like Proverbs. It is the study of a definite experience to which the author devotes himself. The title means "the preacher" and it refers to a man who must have been a great pessimist. He finds much human endeavor quite futile, summing up his philosophy in the words, "Vanity of vanities, all is vanity." He taught the young men of Jerusalem that "all things are full of weariness" and that life has no real meaning. This cynical, worldly book has always been one of the Bible's most popular books with unbelievers. In its words skeptical readers find an echo of many of their own thoughts in moments of gloom. It does, however, contain much wholesome advice and ends with the summons, "Fear God, and keep his commandments; for this is the whole duty of man."

There are two writings, one in the Old Testament and one in the New, that belong to a style of literature peculiar to the Jews. It is called apocalyptic literature. In the Old Testament, it is exemplified by the closing six chapters of the book of Daniel and in the New Testament by the book of Revelation. There are shorter passages of similar writing in Zechariah, Ezekiel, one chapter in each of the gospels and short passages in Paul's letters, especially those to the Thessalonians.

The word "apocalypse" is from the Greek and may be accurately translated as "revelation." The literal meaning of revelation is "the taking off of the veil." The Bible writers employed apocalyptic writing in days of persecution when it was unsafe to speak in plain language. Apocalyptic literature is code literature. The one for whom it is written understands it, but the one against whom it speaks does not.

As pointed out earlier, the book of Daniel was written at the time when Antiochus Epiphanes was trying to substitute his form of religion for that of the Jews, and even went so far as to desecrate the altar of the Temple with the offering of swine. The struggle provoked thereby ended in the wars of the Maccabees and the triumph of the Jews. The last six chapters of Daniel express in coded writing the coming judgment that is to fall on those oppressing the people.

Similarly, the last book of the Bible, "The Revelation of St. John the Divine," is a Christian adaptation of this same kind of writing. John was an exile for his faith on the island of Patmos in the Mediterranean. The Roman Emperor was demanding that every one of his subjects recognize him as god. This the Christians could not do. So John wrote to the leading churches encouraging them to stand firm. His cryptic language they will be able to understand, although it will mean nothing to any Roman officer who may chance to find a copy of it. Its message is one of confidence in the ultimate victory of the Christian faith.

An immense amount of study has been put into the meaning of the Bible's apocalyptic sections, but for the general reader the burden of their message is contained in the words, "The kingdoms of this world are become the kingdoms of our Lord and of his Christ; and he shall reign for ever and ever."

If you plan to delve into the apocalyptic literature, it would be well to do some preliminary study of them in a Bible dictionary or in a guidebook that discusses them in detail.

There remains just one form of literature used in the Bible which has not already been discussed here: personal letters. These are all found in the New Testament and because of their simplicity and directness need little comment. Almost all of Paul's letters are short enough to be read at one sitting. One of the best times for reading them is while you are reading The Acts, since many of the letters are written to congregations in cities mentioned in The Acts.

Because Paul was not successful in proselytizing his fellow Hebrews, the greater part of his whirlwind career was given to winning the gentile world over to the gospel of Christ.

It was to tell these gentiles about Jesus that Paul began his famous journeys which kept him traveling for years. Besides seeing the congregations personally Paul also wrote them, answering questions about the new religion and amplifying important points. In our Bible are more than a dozen such letters, each labeled according to its destination, such as "Paul's Letter to the Romans" or "Paul's Letter to the Ephesians." In each case, however, he is addressing only a handful of the residents of each town. Many of these had become or were soon to become the first Christians in their communities; men and women who embraced the teachings of Paul's Master.

Probably no man who has ever put pen to paper has done more to change the thinking of the world than has Paul. He did it without writing a heavy work of systematic philosophy, but simply by addressing his thoughts to little groups of friends. Nevertheless, Paul's letters are such profound interpretations of the meaning of Christ that countless works of theology have been written to expound them.

Paul's letters still do today what he first intended them to do: they stiffen the backbone of our belief, they remind us that all things are possible if we have faith, and they repeat triumphantly Jesus' gospel of universal love among men.

Besides the letters attributed to Paul, there are eight others in the New Testament, almost all quite short. They reflect the utterly dedicated spirit of the early church fathers and tell us a great deal about the problems they confronted in building the fellowship that would later sweep the world.

While reading these letters you should, whenever possible, keep your Bible dictionary close at hand. This will help you to determine approximately when each letter may have been written and the circumstances of its composition. Such information unfolds the meaning and adds much to the value of these early Christian documents.

We hope that this brief tour through the Old Testament books and through the history- and letter-writing of the New Testament, along with our earlier comments on the four gospels, will give you some inkling of the enormous variety and scope of the Bible's writing. In the truest sense, the Bible has something in it for everybody, a prize for every man and woman who approaches it in the proper spirit. If this were not so, its light would have flickered out ages ago, along with many another ancient book.

Many people ask why the Bible should have so much war, bloodshed and crime in it. The answer is that the early stories of the Hebrew race are honestly told of a people whose chief interest was in discovering the will of their God. They saw him only dimly at first and, like all people, conceived of him in terms of their own limitations. But gradually, mostly through their prophets, they elevated their concept of him and came to know him as a God of forgiveness and love. Naturally, this also helped them become better people themselves.

Christianity teaches that God ultimately revealed himself in the life and teachings and death of Jesus as a God far different than had ever been dreamed of before.

The Bible is the record of this gradual growth: the increasing elevation of men's perception of God and increasing awareness of their duty to one another. It is the only book of its kind in the world.

If this book encourages you to spend only a few additional hours with your Bible, it will have done its work. For we are confident that once you have approached the Bible with such guidance as is offered here, the contagion of Bible reading will capture you itself. And once that happens, once the Bible is as much a part of your daily routine as food or sleep, a great new force will be operating in your life for goodness, for achievement, and for truth.

"Heaven and earth shall pass away, but my words shall not pass away."

Appendices

I The Various Editions of the Bible

Here is a listing of a few special editions of the Bible that are currently available in libraries and bookstores. These books are the work of editors who have labored to present the words of the Bible in formats they felt would most encourage reading. The editions below have proved the soundness of their editors' judgment by winning strong and continuing popularity.

The Reader's Bible. This is a book of almost 2,000 pages which uses the King James Version. It is printed not in two columns but in a single column across the page like most books. It indicates the chapters of the various books of the Bible, but not the verses. It includes all the apocryphal books not usually found in Protestant Bibles. This edition is a little too bulky to be held in the hand comfortably for long periods. It is a beautiful work of publishing, however, and you may enjoy keeping it in your home for occasional reading and reference. Published by Oxford University Press (1951).

The Bible For Today. This is also published by the Oxford University Press (1941). It contains the whole of the Old and New Testaments in the King James Version. The unique feature is its nearly 200 illustrations, all original pen sketches. They are not so much sketches of biblical scenes as pictures of modern life. Through these pictures and their captions (as well as the headings to each book and many sections of the books) the reader is helped to apply his reading to his own problems and the problems of today. For instance, in the middle of II Kings, we find a panoramic photograph of the New York skyline. The caption reads, "Is New York giving a better answer than Jerusalem to the problem of a metropolis?" Below this caption, in smaller type, the reader's thinking is further challenged by these words: "Is it, on the one hand, getting nearer to the solution of the social struggle of its citizens, and on the other, serving mankind by making a stand in the name of the God of freedom and justice in the struggle which is going on between the cities of the world for political and commercial supremacy? In the purpose of God every metropolis has a mission."

The Westminster Bible. This is an excellent Bible for a student. It contains the King James text with helpful notes at the bottom of the pages and introductory prefaces to the various books. It also has colored maps and a concordance. It is published by the Westminster Press.

The Pilgrim Bible. This is a handy-sized, inexpensive Bible in the King James Text. Edited by a group of conservative scholars, it carries explanatory notes attractively arranged at the bottom of the page. It is especially useful for young people. The notes are indexed at the back of the book, enhancing its value for study purposes. There are also introductory chapters to the Old and New Testaments and similar paragraphs at the beginning of each book of the Bible. It is published by the Oxford University Press.

So much for special editions which carry the complete text of the Bible. There are others, of course, but these four have found the greatest response among Bible readers.

Now we come to editions of the Bible which do not present the whole text. Some cutting has been done, of passages which the editors felt were of less interest to the general reader and which—like genealogies, legal codes, repetitious chronicles—might actually hinder his reading. Among these editions where the cutting is carefully and intelligently done, and is not extensive, there are three that might be mentioned here.

The Bible Designed To Be Read As Living Literature. This edition uses the King James Version except for Job, Ecclesiastes, Proverbs and the Song of Songs, where it uses the Revised Version of 1901. It is a beautifully printed volume, in a single column with big, readable type. The books have been somewhat rearranged to reflect the order of their composition whenever possible. The underlying point of view of the edition as expressed by the editor, Ernest Sutherland Bates, is to present not all the Bible but the best of it, for literary appreciation. Prose is printed as prose and poetry as poetry. Modern paragraphing and punctuation are used throughout. The emphasis is on readability and enjoyment, and in this the edition succeeds very well. Published by Simon and Schuster.

The Home Bible is similar to the edition just described. It has many of the same aims; uses the King James Version throughout. It is also illustrated with thirty-six pictures and designs by William Blake and with interesting thumbnail sketches in the margins. The editor is Ruth Hornblower Greenough. Published by Harper and Brothers (1950).

The Dartmouth Bible is the most recent of these larger edited Bibles, and describes itself as "an abridgement of the King James Version with aids to its understanding as history and literature and as a source of religious experience." It contains parts of the Apocrypha and is particularly helpful in its introduction and prefaces to the various books, and its notes and maps. It was prepared by two Dartmouth College professors with the counsel of an advisory board of American biblical scholars. Published by Harper.

From these editions with minor cuts in the text we go on to editions with extensive cuts.

The Compact Bible, published by Hawthorn Books, reduces the King James text to less than 500 pages of good, readable one-column paragraphs. The editor has attempted to keep as many as possible of the best-loved, most widely known and most significant passages.

The Short Bible is another abbreviated Bible. This is a condensation of *The Bible: An American Translation* made by two of the original translators, Dr. Edgar J. Goodspeed and Dr. J. M. P. Smith. Published by the University of Chicago Press.

II A Reference-List to the Stories of the Bible

STORIES OF THE OLD TESTAMENT

EARLY BEGINNINGS

Creation and Sin	*Genesis 2:4-3:24*
The First Murder	*Genesis 4:1-15*
Noah and the Flood	*Genesis 6:1-9:17*
The Tower of Babel	*Genesis 11:1-9*
The Destruction of Sodom and Gomorrah and of Lot's Wife	*Genesis 19:1-28*
Abraham's Offering of Isaac	*Genesis 22:1-19*
The Story of Jacob	*Genesis 25:19-35:29*
The Story of Joseph	*Genesis 37-50*
Moses: In Egypt	*Exodus 1-14*
Wilderness Wanderings	*Exodus 15:22-20:26; 31:18-34:35; Numbers 20-21:25*
Farewell and Death	*Deuteronomy 31-34*
Balaam and Balak	*Numbers 22-24*

WAR STORIES

Rahab and Red Thread	*Joshua 2*
Joshua, Military Strategist	*Joshua 3; 6; 8*
The Defeat of Sisera	*Judges 4:4-24*
Gideon, the Conqueror	*Judges 6:11-8:32*
The Parable of Jotham	*Judges 9:7-21*
The Daughter of Jephthah	*Judges 11:1-11, 29-40*
The Story of Samson	*Judges 13:24-16:31*

NATIONAL HISTORY

The Story of Ruth	*Ruth 1-4*
The Story of Samuel	*I Samuel 1-3; 7-10; 12; 15; 16*
Saul, the First King	*I Samuel 8-11; 13; 15; 28; 31*
David, the Shepherd King	*I Samuel 16-27; 29-30:25*
II Samuel 9; 11; 12; 15:1-18; 18; I Kings 1:1-31; 2:1-11	
King Solomon	*I Kings 2:12-11:43*
Elijah, Great Prophet	*I Kings 17-19; 21; II Kings 1*
Elisha, His Successor	*II Kings 2; 4-6; 13:14-21*
Jehu's Triumph Over Jezebel	*II Kings 9*
Nehemiah, Heroic Builder	*Nehemiah 1; 2; 4*
Esther, Queenly Heroine	*Esther 1:9-7:10*
Shadrach, Meshach and Abednego	*Daniel 3*
Belshazzar's Feast and the Handwriting on the Wall	
	Daniel 5
Daniel in the Lion's Den	*Daniel 6*
Jonah, Reluctant Missionary	*Jonah 1-4*

STORIES OF THE GOSPELS

JOHN THE BAPTIST

His Ministry	*Matthew 3; Mark 1:1-11; Luke 3:1-20*
His Execution by Herod	*Matthew 14:1-12; Mark 6:14-29*

THE LIFE OF JESUS

The Birth of Jesus	*Matthew 1:18-2:15; Luke 1:5-2:40*
The Young Jesus	*Luke 2:41-52*
The Baptism of Jesus	
	Matthew 3; Mark 1:1-11; Luke 3:21, 22
The Temptation of Jesus	
	Matthew 4:1-11; Mark 1:12, 13; Luke 4:1-13
The Sermon on the Mount	*Matthew 5-7; Luke 6:20-49*

MIRACLES OF JESUS

The Healing of a Leper
                    Matthew 8:1-4; Mark 1:40-45; Luke 5:12-16
The Centurion's Servant   *Matthew 8:5-13; Luke 7:1-10*
The Healing of Peter's Wife's Mother
                    Matthew 8:14, 15; Mark 1:29-31; Luke 4:38, 39
The Calming of the Tempest
                    Matthew 8:23-27; Mark 4:35-41; Luke 8:22-25
The Demoniacs of Gadara
                    Matthew 8:28-34; Mark 5:1-20; Luke 8:26-39
The Man with the Palsy
                    Matthew 9:1-8; Mark 2:1-12; Luke 5:17-26
The Daughter of Jairus and the Woman with an Issue
                    Matthew 9:18-26; Mark 5:21-43; Luke 8:40-56
The Two Blind Men   *Matthew 9:27-31*
The Man with the Dumb Spirit   *Matthew 9:32-34*
The Man with a Withered Hand
                    Matthew 12:9-14; Mark 3:1-6; Luke 6:6-11
The Demoniac
                Matthew 12:22-37; Mark 3:20-30; Luke 11:14-23
The Feeding of the Five Thousand
        Matthew 14:13-23; Mark 6:30-46; Luke 9:10-17; John 6:1-15
The Daughter of the Woman of Canaan
                            Matthew 15:21-28; Mark 7:24-30
The Feeding of the Four Thousand
                            Matthew 15:32-39; Mark 8:1-9
The Boy Possessed of a Devil
                    Matthew 17:14-21; Mark 9:14-29; Luke 9:37-43
Two Blind Men
                Matthew 20:29-34; Mark 10:46-52; Luke 18:35-43
The Fig Tree   *Matthew 21:18-22; Mark 11:12-14*
Another Demoniac   *Mark 1:21-28; Luke 4:31-37*
The Deaf and Dumb Man   *Mark 7:31-37*
The Draught of Fishes   *Luke 5:1-11*
The Widow's Son   *Luke 7:11-17*
The Woman Healed on the Sabbath   *Luke 13:10-17*
The Man with the Dropsy   *Luke 14:1-6*
The Ten Lepers Cleansed   *Luke 17:11-19*

PARABLES OF JESUS

The Pharisee and the Publican   *Luke 18:9-14*
The Pounds   *Luke 19:11-27*

THE TRIUMPH OF JESUS

> *Matthew 21:1-11; Mark 11:1-11; Luke 19:29-44;*
> *John 12:12-19*

THE LAST SUPPER OF JESUS

> *Matthew 26:17-35; Mark 14:12-26; Luke 22:1-38*

THE AGONY OF JESUS IN GETHSEMANE

> *Matthew 26:36-46; Mark 14:32-42; Luke 22:39-46*

THE CRUCIFIXION OF JESUS

> *Matthew 26:47-27:66; Mark 14:43-15:47;*
> *Luke 22:47-23:56; John 18; 19*

THE RESURRECTION OF JESUS

> *Matthew 28:1-10; Mark 16; Luke 24:1-12; John 20*

OTHER NEW TESTAMENT STORIES

The Ascension of Jesus   *Acts 1:1-12*
The Pentecost   *Acts 2*
Stephen, the First Martyr   *Acts 6:5-15; 7:54-60*
Philip and the Ethiopian   *Acts 8:26-39*
Saul of Tarsus   *Acts 9:1-32*
Peter and Cornelius   *Acts 10*
Peter in Prison   *Acts 12:1-19*
Paul in Prison   *Acts 16:16-40*
The Riot at Ephesus   *Acts 19:23-41*
Paul's Voyage to Rome   *Acts 27; 28*

III A Reference-List to the Poetry of the Bible

In the Beginning	*Genesis 1-2:7*
Horse and Rider in the Sea, Moses' Song of Deliverance	*Exodus 15:1-19*
Honey Out of the Rock, Farewell of Moses	*Deuteronomy 32:1-43*
War in the Gates, Hymn of Deborah	*Judges 5:1-31*
The Pillars of the Earth, Song of Hannah	*I Samuel 2:1-10*
Let There Be No Dew, Lament of David	*II Samuel 1:19-27*
Who Am I and What Is My House? Prayer of David	*II Samuel 7:18-29*
There Is None Else, Prayer of Solomon	*I Kings 8:22-61*
From Nation to Nation, Hymn of David	*I Chronicles 16:7-36*

FROM THE PSALMS

Hymn of Righteousness	*Psalm 1*
Hymn to God the Maker	*Psalm 8*
Hymn of Salvation	*Psalm 18*
Hymn to the Creator	*Psalm 19*
Hymn to the Good Shepherd	*Psalm 23*
Hymn to the Lord	*Psalm 24*
Hymn of Confidence	*Psalm 27*
Hymn of Trust	*Psalm 37*
Hymn of Hope	*Psalm 42*

Hymn to the Omnipotent	*Psalm 46*
Hymn of Penitence	*Psalm 51*
Hymn of the Nations	*Psalm 67*
Hymn for Success	*Psalm 90*
Hymn to God, the Almighty	*Psalm 91*
Hymn of Glory to God	*Psalm 96*
Hymn of Thanksgiving	*Psalm 103*
Hymn to the Great Watchman	*Psalm 121*
Hymn to the Native Land	*Psalm 137*
Hymn of Praise	*Psalm 150*

FROM THE SONG OF SOLOMON

Rise Up, My Love	*Song of Songs 2:10-17*
I Sought Him	*Song of Songs 3:1-5*
If You Find My Beloved	*Song of Songs 5:1-8*
A Seal Upon Thine Heart	*Song of Songs 8:6, 7*

FROM JOB

A Vein for Silver	*Job 28*
Answer Thou Me	*Job 38, 39*
Behemoth and Leviathan	*Job 40:6-41:34*

FROM ISAIAH

There Shall Be No End	*Isaiah 9:2-7*
The Wolf and the Lamb	*Isaiah 11:1-9*
Sorrow and Sighing Shall Flee Away	*Isaiah 34, 35*
Have You Not Known?	*Isaiah 40*
The Man of Sorrows	*Isaiah 53*
Milk Without Money	*Isaiah 55*
Beauty for Ashes	*Isaiah 61:1-6*

FROM OTHER PROPHETS

Clay in the Potter's Hand	*Jeremiah 18:1-17*
Bright the Arrows	*Jeremiah 51:10-58*

IV Wisdom from the Bible

Wisdom	*Job 28:12-38; Psalms 111:10;*
	Proverbs 3:13-18; 4:5-9; 12:1;
	Ecclesiastes 9:13-18; James 1:5-7
Devotion to God	*Proverbs 3:1-7; 9:10;*
	Jeremiah 9:23, 24; Hosea 14:9; Micah 6:6-8
The Law of God	*Deuteronomy 6:1-9;*
	Jeremiah 8:7-9; Matthew 7:24-27
Justice	*Proverbs 3:27-31; 4:18, 19; 21:23; Amos 5:21-24*
Industry	*Proverbs 6:6-8; 10:4, 5; 21:5;*
	22:29; 24:30-32; Ecclesiastes 3:13
Wealth	*Proverbs 11:4, 27-31;*
	15:16, 17; 22:1, 2, 4
Kindness	*Proverbs 14:21; 21:13; 25:21, 22;*
	Matthew 5:24; Romans 12:20
Use of the Tongue	*Proverbs 13:3; 15:1-4;*
	16:24; James 3:3-13
Cheerfulness	*Proverbs 12:25; 15:13, 15; 17:22*
Friendliness	*Proverbs 10:12; 17:9, 17; 18:24; 28:23*
Youth	*Ecclesiastes 11:9 to 12:14*
Modesty	*Proverbs 11:2, 14; 16:18*
A Time for All Things	*Ecclesiastes 3:1-8*
The Love of God	*John 3:1-21*
Fellowship with Christ	*John 14*
Christian Brotherhood	*John 15:1-13*
The Nature of God	*Acts 17:22-31*
The Law of the Spirit	*Romans 8;*
	1 Corinthians 2:9-14
Happiness	*Romans 12*

V Men and Women of the Bible

MEN OF THE BIBLE

ADAM, THE FIRST OF ALL

CAIN AND ABEL

NOAH, THE FIRST SAILOR

ABRAHAM, THE FATHER OF HIS PEOPLE

JACOB, THE POLITICIAN

Jacob's brother Esau	*Genesis 27:30-45*
Jacob's dream	*Genesis 28:10-22*
Jacob's wrestling-match	*Genesis 32:24-32*
Jacob's meeting with Esau	*Genesis 33:1-17*

JOSEPH, SLAVE AND STATESMAN

Joseph, father's favorite	*Genesis 37:3-11*
Joseph, the slave	*Genesis 37:12-36*
Joseph, the reader of dreams	*Genesis 41:9-24*
Joseph, the prime minister	*Genesis 41:25-40*
Joseph, the brother	*Genesis 42:1-8*
Joseph, the son	*Genesis 46:28-47:11*

MOSES, FOUNDER OF A NATION

From slave to prince	*Exodus 2:1-10*
The burning bush	*Exodus 3:1-12*
The Tenth Plague	*Exodus 11:1-8*
The Passover	*Exodus 12:21-34*
The Hebrews pursued	*Exodus 14:5-14*
The Hebrews escape	*Exodus 14:19-31*
The Ten Commandments	*Exodus 20:1-17*

JOSHUA, CONQUEROR OF CANAAN

Joshua succeeds Moses	*Joshua 1:1-11*
The walls of Jericho	*Joshua 6:1-5*

GIDEON, FOUR-STAR GENERAL	*Judges 7:12-23*

SAMSON, THE STRONG MAN

His strength	*Judges 16:1-17*
His weakness	*Judges 16:18-31*

SAMUEL, THE LAST OF THE JUDGES

The call in the night	*I Samuel 3:1-21*
Samuel chooses a king	*I Samuel 16:1-13*

DAVID, FROM SLINGSHOT TO THRONE

Challenged	*I Samuel 17:2-11*
Shepherd	*I Samuel 17:31-40*
Victor	*I Samuel 17:41-51*
Monarch	*II Samuel 5:1-5; 7:18-29*
Poet	*II Samuel 22:1-20*
Leader	*I Kings 2:1-4*

JONATHAN, A HERO FRIEND

David and Jonathan	*I Samuel 20:1-17*

SOLOMON, WEALTHY AND WISE

The test of a wise man	*I Kings 3:16-28*
The Temple that Solomon built	*I Kings 6:2-4, 11-22*

ELIJAH, THE GREAT PROPHET

Bread in famine	*I Kings 17:1-16*
Elijah's victory	*I Kings 18:20-40*
The still, small voice	*I Kings 19:9-18*

THE TROUBLES OF JOB

All or nothing	*Job 1:1-22*
Friends in need	*Job 2:11, 3:10*
Yearns for God	*Job 23:1-17*
Out of the whirlwind	*Job 38:1-18*
Happily ever after	*Job 42:7-17*

JEREMIAH, HEROIC PATRIOT

His Call	*Jeremiah 1:4-10*

DANIEL VERSUS THE PAGANS   *Daniel 6:4-23*

THE TRAVELS OF JONAH

Retreat   *Jonah 1*
Reaction   *Jonah 2; 3*
Repentance   *Jonah 4*

JOHN THE BAPTIST, DESERT PREACHER   *Matthew 3:1-12*

JESUS, THE SON OF GOD

His birth   *Matthew 2:1-12*
His Temptation   *Matthew 4:1-11*
His Sermon on the Mount   *Matthew 5:1-1-16*
His parable: The Prodigal Son   *Luke 15:11-32*
His miracle: Cleansing the Lepers   *Luke 17:11-19*
His entrance into Jerusalem   *Luke 19:28-40*
His Last Supper   *Luke 22:7-20*
His Crucifixion   *Matthew 27:24-50*
His Resurrection   *Matthew 28:1-10*

PETER, FEAR INTO FAITH

Little faith   *Matthew 14:22-33*
No! No! No!   *Luke 22:54-62*
More than silver or gold   *Acts 3:1-10*
Escape   *Acts 12:1-11*

PAUL, RELIGIOUS PIONEER

From Jerusalem   *Acts 9:1-9*
To Damascus   *Acts 9:10-28*
In Lystra   *Acts 14:8-22*
Beaten and imprisoned   *Acts 16:16-34*
Across the Mediterranean   *Acts 27:1, 2, 14-26*
West to Rome   *Acts 27:27-44*

WOMEN OF THE BIBLE

EVE, THE FIRST WOMAN	*Genesis 2:18-25*
SARAH, PRINCESS-MOTHER	
Princess	*Genesis 17:15-21*
Mother	*Genesis 21:1-8*
HAGAR, A REFUGEE	*Genesis 21:9-21*
REBEKAH, THE BEAUTIFUL	
By the well	*Genesis 24:15-28*
Going home	*Genesis 24:55-67*
RACHEL, SEVEN YEARS' WORTH	*Genesis 29:9-20*
MIRIAM, SISTER OF MOSES	
Jealous of her brother	*Numbers 12:1-15*
DEBORAH AND JAEL, WARRIOR-WOMEN	*Judges 4:4-9, 15-23*
RUTH, LOVE'S LABORS WON	
Whither thou goest	*Ruth 1:1-18*
A measure of barley	*Ruth 2:1-14*
Mother of a king	*Ruth 4:9-17*
HANNAH, THE SINGER	
Her son	*I Samuel 1:9-20, 24-28*
Her song	*I Samuel 2:1-10*
THE QUEEN OF SHEBA	*II Chronicles 9:1-12*

ESTHER, THE HEBREW JOAN OF ARC

The new queen	*Esther 2:15-20; 3:1-6*
Mass Murder Planned	*Esther 3:8-11*
The Queen's banquet	*Esther 5:1-9*
The Queen's triumph	*Esther 7:1-10*

ELIZABETH, THE PRIEST'S WIFE   *Luke 1:5-7, 24, 25, 41-45*

THE VIRGIN MARY, MOTHER OF JESUS

The Annunciation	*Luke 1:26-38*
The Magnificat	*Luke 1:46-55*
The Nativity	*Luke 2:1-19*

MARY AND MARTHA

Work and Worship	*Luke 10:38-42*
Mary's Anointing	*John 12:1-8*

MARY MAGDALENE, THE SCARLET LILY   *John 20:1-3, 11-18*

THE WIDOW'S MITE   *Mark 12:41-44*

THE WOMAN WITH THE ISSUE OF BLOOD   *Luke 8:43-48*

THE WOMAN OF SAMARIA   *John 4:5-30*

A WOMAN OF CANAAN   *Matthew 15:21-28*

THE MOTHER OF JAMES AND JOHN

Favors for her sons	*Matthew 20:20-28*

THREE EARLY CONVERTS

Dorcas	*Acts 9:36-42*
Lydia	*Acts 16:14, 15*
Priscilla	*Acts 18:1-3, 18-26*

VI A Reference-List to Songs, Prayers and Benedictions of the Bible

SOME SONGS OF THE BIBLE

Moses' Song of Deliverance	*Exodus 15:1-19*
Moses' Farewell	*Deuteronomy 31:30-32:47*
The Song of Deborah	*Judges 5:1-31*
The Song of Hannah	*I Samuel 2:1-10*
David's Lament	*II Samuel 1:17-27*
David's Song of Deliverance	*II Samuel 22*
The Song of David	*I Chronicles 16:7-36*
The Symphony of the Heavens	*Psalms 8*
The Lord, My Shepherd and Host	*Psalms 23*
The Entrance of the King	*Psalms 24*
God's Beauty in the Morning	*Psalms 27*
Confidence in God's Present Help	*Psalms 46*
The Protection of the Man Who Trusts	*Psalms 91*
A Song for the Sabbath Day	*Psalms 92*
The Floods of Chaos	*Psalms 93*
God's Voice Today	*Psalms 95*
The King Who Has Come	*Psalms 96*
A Dread and Fearsome King	*Psalms 97*
The Wonderful Acclaim of the World	*Psalms 98*
A Challenge of Righteous Rule	*Psalms 99*
Enter His Gates Singing	*Psalms 100*
A Heart of Praise	*Psalms 103*

248

Creator, Provider, Sustainer	*Psalms 104*
Vows of Thanksgiving	*Psalms 107*
Worthy of Great Praise	*Psalms 145*
The God of Nature	*Psalms 147*
All Nature Sings	*Psalms 148*
A Paean of Praise	*Psalms 150*
Solomon's Love Song	*Song of Solomon 2:10-17*
The Magnificat of Mary	*Luke 1:46-55*
The Benedictus	*Luke 1:68-79*
The Nunc Dimittis	*Luke 2:29-32*

PRAYERS OF THE BIBLE

Solomon's Personal Prayer	*I Kings 3:5-10*
Solomon's Public Prayer	
	I Kings 8:22-61; II Chronicles 6:12-42
Hezekiah's Temple Prayer	*II Kings 19:15-20*
	Isaiah 37:14-20
David's Prayer of Thanksgiving	*I Chronicles 29:10-19*
A Morning Insight	*Psalms 5*
The Searcher of Hearts	*Psalms 7*
Practising the Presence	*Psalms 16*
Praise to Him	*Psalms 22*
Hungry for God's Intimacy	*Psalms 25*
Helped and Rejuvenated	*Psalms 28*
In God's Hand	*Psalms 31*
Wait for God	*Psalms 42*
A Cry for Cleansing and Pardon	*Psalms 51*
God Upholds My Soul	*Psalms 54*
Cast Thy Burden	*Psalms 55*
In Grave Peril	*Psalms 57*
Shelter in God	*Psalms 61*
Thirsty for God	*Psalms 63*
An Appeal for Help	*Psalms 64*
Seeing God's Hand	*Psalms 71*
Expecting a Gracious Sign	*Psalms 86*
God, Our Eternal Home	*Psalms 90*
A Cry Out of the Depths	*Psalms 130*
Life Examined by God	*Psalms 139*

Satisfied in the Morning	*Psalms 143*
Happiness from God	*Psalms 144*
Jeremiah's Prayer	*Jeremiah 32:16-24*
Daniel's Prayer	*Daniel 9:3-19*
Jonah's Prayer	*Jonah 2:1-9*
The Lord's Prayer	*Matthew 6:9-13*
Jesus' Prayer in Gethsemane	*Matthew 26:36-44*
Prayers of the Pharisee and the Publican	*Luke 18:9-14*
The Thief's Prayer	*Luke 23:42*
Jesus' Prayer for His Disciples	*John 17*
The Disciples' Prayer	*Acts 4:24-31*
Paul's Thanks for Timothy	*II Timothy 1:3-7*

BIBLE BENEDICTIONS AND BLESSINGS

"The Lord watch" (Mizpah)	*Genesis 31:49*
"The Lord make his face to shine upon thee" (Aaronic)	
	Numbers 6:24-26
"The Lord our God be with us" (Solomon)	
	I Kings 8:57, 58
"Let the words of my mouth"	*Psalms 19:14*
"The God of patience"	*Romans 15:5, 6, 13, 33*
"Now to Him that is of power"	*Romans 16:25-27*
"Grace be unto you"	*I Corinthians 1:3*
"The grace of our Lord Jesus Christ"	*II Corinthians 13:14*
"Peace be to the brethren"	*Ephesians 6:23, 24*
"The Peace of God"	*Philippians 4:7-9*
"May our God count you worthy"	
	II Thessalonians 1:11, 12
"Now the Lord of peace"	*II Thessalonians 3:16, 18*
"Grace, mercy and peace"	*I Timothy 1:2*
"The God of peace"	*Hebrews 13:20, 21*
"The God of all grace"	*I Peter 5:10, 11, 14*
"Grace be with you"	*II John 3*
"Now unto Him that is able to keep you"	*Jude 2, 24, 25*
"Unto Him that loved us"	*Revelation 1:4-6*

VII Where to Look in the Bible

WHEN . . .

Desiring inward peace — *John 14; Romans 8*

Everything is going well — *Psalms 33:12-22; 100; I Timothy 6; James 2:1-17*

Satisfied with yourself — *Proverbs 11; Luke 16*

Seeking the best investment — *Matthew 7*

Starting a new job — *Psalms 1; Proverbs 16; Philippians 3:7-21*

You have been placed in a position of responsibility — *Joshua 1:1-9; Proverbs 2; II Corinthians 8:1-15*

Making a new home — *Psalms 127; Proverbs 17; Ephesians 5; Colossians 3; I Peter 3:1-17; I John 4*

You are out for a good time — *Matthew 15:1-20; II Corinthians 3; Galatians 5*

Wanting to live successfully with your fellow men — *Romans 12*

Anxious for dear ones — *Psalms 121; Luke 17*

Business is poor — *Psalms 37, 92; Ecclesiastes 5*

Discouraged — *Psalms 23, 42, 43*

Everything seems to be going from bad to worse — *II Timothy 3; Hebrews 13*

Friends seem to go back on you — *Matthew 5; I Corinthians 13*

Sorrow overtakes you — *Psalms 46; Matthew 28*

Tempted to do wrong — *Psalms 15, 19, 139; Matthew 4; James 1*

Things look "blue" — *Psalms 34, 71; Isaiah 40*

You seem too busy — *Ecclesiastes 3:1-15*

You can't go to sleep — *Psalms 4, 56, 130*

You have quarreled   *Matthew 18; Ephesians 4; James 4*
You are weary   *Psalms 95:1-7; Matthew 11*
Worries oppress you   *Psalms 46; Matthew 6*

IF YOU . . .

Are challenged by opposing forces

Ephesians 6; Philippians 4
Are facing a crisis   *Job 28:12-28; Proverbs 8; Isaiah 55*
Are jealous   *Psalms 49; James 3*
Are impatient   *Psalms 40, 90; Hebrews 12*
Are bereaved   *I Corinthians 15;*
I Thessalonians 4:13-5:28; Revelation 21, 22
Are bored   *II Kings 5; Job 38; Psalms 103, 104;*
Ephesians 3
Bear a grudge   *Luke 6; II Corinthians 4; Ephesians 4*
Have experienced severe losses   *Colossians 1; I Peter 1*
Have been disobedient   *Isaiah 6; Mark 12; Luke 5*
Need forgiveness   *Matthew 23; Luke 15; Philemon*
Are sick or in pain   *Psalms 6, 39, 41, 67; Isaiah 26*

WHEN YOU . . .

Feel your faith is weak   *Psalms 126, 146; Hebrews 11*
Think God seems far away   *Psalms 25, 125, 138; Luke 10*
Are leaving home   *Psalms 119; Proverbs 3, 4*
Are planning your budget   *Mark 4; Luke 19*
Are becoming lax and indifferent

Matthew 25; Revelation 3
Are lonely or fearful   *Psalms 27, 91; Luke 8; I Peter 4*
Fear death   *John 11, 17, 20; II Corinthians 5;*
I John 3; Revelation 14
Have sinned   *Psalms 51; Isaiah 53; John 3; I John 1*
Want to know the way of prayer

I Kings 8:12-61; Luke 11, 18
Want a worshipful mood   *Psalms 24, 84, 116;*
Isaiah 1:10-20; John 4:1-45
Are concerned with God in national life

Deuteronomy 8; Psalms 85, 118, 124;
Isaiah 41:8-20; Micah 4, 6:6-16

Places of the
OLD
TESTAMENT

TO GREECE
• Sidon
Mt. Hermon
Damascus •
TO BABYLONIA
AND ASSYRIA
• Tyre
SYRIA
• Dan
LAKE
MEROM
SEA OF
CHINNERETH
PHOENICIANS
SYRIA
ISRAEL
Mt. Carmel
ESDRAELON OR
VALLEY OF JEZREEL
Mt. Gilboa
RIVER JORDAN
Plain of Sharon
MEDITERRANEAN SEA
ISRAEL
Shechem •
AMMONITES
• Joppa
Bethel
Jericho •
ISRAEL
JUDAH
PHILISTINES
• Ekron
Jerusalem •
Bethlehem •
• Ashdod
• Ashkelon
JUDAH
DEAD SEA
Hebron •
• Gaza
JUDAH
MOABITES
Beersheba •
TO MT. SINAI
TO EGYPT
EDOMITES

253

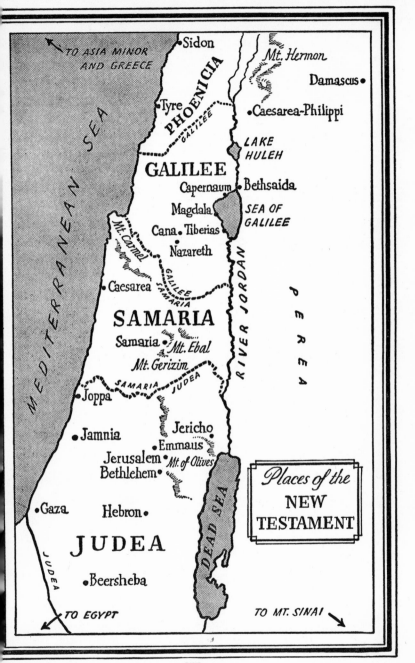

TO ASIA MINOR AND GREECE

• Sidon

MEDITERRANEAN SEA

PHOENICIA

• Tyre

Mt. Hermon

Damascus •

• Caesarea-Philippi

GALILEE

LAKE HULEH

Capernaum • Bethsaida

Magdala

SEA OF GALILEE

Mt. Carmel

Cana • Tiberias

Nazareth

GALILEE
SAMARIA

• Caesarea

SAMARIA

Samaria • Mt. Ebal

Mt. Gerizim

RIVER JORDAN

PEREA

SAMARIA

JUDEA

• Joppa

• Jamnia

Jericho •

Emmaus •

Jerusalem • Mt. of Olives

Bethlehem

DEAD SEA

• Gaza

Hebron •

Places of the
NEW
TESTAMENT

JUDEA

• Beersheba

JUDEA

TO EGYPT

TO MT. SINAI